REALTORS®

WHAT'S HOLDING BACK YOUR CAREER IS YOU

THE PROVEN PROCESS THAT WILL TRIPLE YOUR INCOME

Brian Crawley

ISBN paperback: 9781954759046
ISBN hardcover: 9781954759039
ISBN ebook: 9781954759053
Published by Cranberry Press
Distributed by National Book Network

Printed in the United States of America.

For more information and inquiries address
Cranberry Press, 110 E. Houston Street, 7th Floor,
San Antonio, TX 78205 or call 210-753-1999

INDEX

Foreword
Marshall Goldsmith

As a leadership expert who has guided countless professionals towards greater success, I recognize a unique opportunity when I see it. **REALTORS®: What's Holding Back Your Career Is You** is precisely that – a game-changer, not just in your real estate career, but in every aspect of your life.

Brian and I share a common philosophy regarding personal development and business success. The skills you'll acquire from this book go beyond mere business tactics — they are transformative tools for personal relationships and future growth in every facet of your life.

In a world where many authors offer advice without the credentials to back it up, Brian Crawley stands apart. His track record of starting over ten companies, selling hundreds of homes, and coaching numerous realtors – many of whom have risen to the top of their markets – speaks volumes. This isn't just theoretical knowledge. It's wisdom born from real-world success.

This book is for realtors, at any career stage. Whether you're struggling to close your first deal, or you're an experienced agent seeking the next level or a better quality of life, Brian's insights are invaluable. His practical tips and profound mental shifts can revolutionize your approach to real estate, as well as to living your life successfully and triumphantly.

Commitment is key. Engage deeply with the activities and lessons in these pages, and I firmly believe you will double or triple your business and enhance your quality of life. This isn't about passive reading. It's about active transformation of your techniques in the real estate world and in your life.

If you're skeptical, wondering if this book rehashes the same old principles, let me assure you: Brian's methods are unique. He has helped countless agents not just succeed, but thrive by leveraging their personal strengths and passions, moving away from stale scripts and one-size-fits-all strategies.

As someone who has coached hundreds of successful entrepreneurs and CEOs, I see the tremendous value in this book. It's not just a guide to succeeding in real estate — it's a blueprint for transforming your life.

I urge you to see and experience its potential and its power for yourself.

- Dr. Marshall Goldsmith is the *Thinkers50* #1 Executive Coach and New York Times bestselling author of *The Earned Life*, *Triggers*, and *What Got You Here Won't Get You There.*

Introduction

Do you limit yourself?

I used to.

But I have learned how to break out of my self-imposed limits. And I've taught many people how to free themselves from what's been holding them back.

As a result of overcoming how they self-sabotage, many of the REALTORS® I work with have become more successful in their careers, happier in their lives and, in many cases, have become financially independent.

Getting past your self-limiting beliefs is not some guarded secret. There's a method to expand your thinking and your point of view, and I will share it with you in these pages.

It's a matter of identifying negative patterns within yourself, where you engage in demeaning self-talk, where you hold yourself back because you actually fear success, subconsciously. You'll find out what holds you back, and why. Also, you will learn how to think big about where you see yourself in the years ahead.

Unfortunately, many people don't know how to identify and change their negative patterns. Neither do they have a strategy for envisioning a future where they succeed.

In this book, you will get the steps to master both of those, because I have discovered how to put these sets of steps together, and how to teach them to you.

Before I could build up my own business in real estate and coaching, I had to discover what was slowing me down in my career. I had to figure out why I sometimes didn't do as well as I hoped. I needed to discover why some deals didn't come together as I anticipated they would. I needed to figure out why I wasn't further along than I wanted to be. I worked with a coach, who helped me find my weak spots. I looked within and saw how some of my family experiences growing up affected my view of myself, and stifled my own potential.

I also discovered methods to organize my day so that I could work more efficiently. I created processes to ensure that I didn't miss out on important sales opportunities. I also learned how to develop my friendships with clients in a way that they also helped my business, and vice versa. I found out that if you can cultivate clients in a certain way, and you treat them as friends, they very often become friends, and your work becomes so much more enjoyable.

Most important, perhaps, I learned to think big.

With this book, you will move through creating goals for your future self. Not small goals, but grand ones that will mean you will need a much higher income than your current one. This is one of your goals: to earn more.

You will also learn tools and approaches for improving your frame of mind as a REALTOR®, and methods and tips on how you can go efficiently and effectively about your workday.

Ultimately, you will learn to believe in yourself!

This is essential to success in all areas of life. Too many of us have lost that belief. We get distracted. We become downhearted. We belittle our own talents. We play the victim. But you are not a victim, which is why you are reading this book. You want to succeed, and this book will help you do just that. Not just as a REALTOR®, but in living your life, generally.

You are worth it!

You can and will do much more than you had ever thought possible.

You will recognize where you have been stuck in your business, and even in your life, because you have been limiting yourself, and you have been unwilling to go out of your comfort zone and try new things. My hope is that this book is the beginning of the end of the hold that those long-held, self-limiting beliefs have had on you.

You have a great future ahead of you.

So turn the page, and we'll begin this exciting journey together, starting right now!

Chapter 1

What's Holding You Back Is... You

You are holding yourself back.

I've seen it so often, I know it's real, no exceptions.

Many people, even those who are already pretty successful, can find it hard to push past their own resistance to further success. They simply don't realize they are their own biggest obstacle.

First, I'm going to tell you about someone who realized he was underestimating himself, and who became much more successful after visualizing a more positive future.

Then I'll provide you with a process for beginning to break out of that negative, self-inflicted holding pattern.

We all have limiting beliefs.

Those who are living paycheck to paycheck are often the ones who hold themselves back the most. You can understand this mindset with salespeople, since many of them think, "How in the world can I make enough sales to pay my bills next month?" Their mindset is focused on how they can get by. They rarely focus on how they can excel and thrive.

Even some agents I know who make $300,000 to $400,000 a

year are holding themselves back in different categories. They make good money, but greater success eludes them. When presented with new opportunities they ask themselves: Is this worth my time if I'm just going to mess it up? Or if I'm going to be uncomfortable doing it? Why would I bother when I'm already making plenty of money?
I'm going to help you overcome the paycheck-to-paycheck mindset and achieve true financial independence. Or, if you're in the second category, I'm going to show you why you should bother, and why it doesn't matter how much money you make, and help you achieve an even-higher level of success.

Inconsistent Networking

I met Owen about five years into his real-estate career. He was making decent money, but despite earning over $100,000 the previous year (quite a bit of money at the time), he was still struggling and almost lost his home about six months before I started working with him.

So Owen hired me to help him improve his business earnings. We started out by doing a detailed analysis of how he was currently making his money.

He had been working very aggressively with investors who wanted to flip homes. Owen would meet new investors at investment seminars, and he would actively search the multiple listings service for good home-flipping opportunities. On the side, he would work his Sphere of Influence a little bit, but he was very scattered and inconsistent in doing so.

On a scale of 1 to 100, Owen was only at 15 in his time working his Sphere of Influence.

The interesting thing was that, although Owen spun his wheels for 50-70 hours a week trying to find investment properties and new investors, and only about 10 hours a week on Sphere of Influence, his income breakdown was about 50-50: 50% came from his Sphere of Influence and 50% from his

investors. The solution seemed obvious to me — I told Owen he needed to spend more time on his Sphere of Influence. He needed to invite previous clients over for dinner, host movie events, and — here's the important, new part — make daily invites to friends and family.
This was easier said than done. Early on in his career, Owen had to force himself to become good at working with investors because that was the only opportunity presenting itself. Because of this forced growth in that specific area, he became very proficient at it and was comfortable working with investors. Owen would meet someone and quickly direct the conversation to real estate investing. He began educating them and getting them excited about investing in real estate. He was very good at this.

But the idea of calling friends and family (his Sphere of Influence or SOI) and simply shooting the breeze was too open-ended for him. Owen did not know where to direct the conversation, or how to move a conversation forward when it stalled. He didn't even know how to *start* a conversation with friends and family.

He asked me, "What in the world am I going to talk about? I can't just call them up and wait for them to talk." So, as a starting point, Owen and I created a strategy for him to hold multiple client events every year, and he would simply invite friends and family to each event. At these events, he wouldn't have to hold long conversations with family or friends. His conversations with them would happen organically, starting when people arrived. Owen used an extremely basic script such as, "Thank you for coming. It's great to see you," as people filed past him.

Later, he would talk with family and friends about other people at the event, recounting the interesting things they were saying that they wanted in real estate, as well as the good real estate decisions they were making. This stimulated their curiosity, and they just naturally began asking questions about those clients and bingo! There he was, talking lots of real estate with family and friends, which eventually led to several sales — mission accomplished!

I also introduced Owen to the Money List (will explain later). I began to categorize his contacts in a way that helped him know whom to contact, and when. I also gave him a list of things to talk about with contacts, as well as some sales clincher techniques.

It took longer than I would have liked to get started on it, but eventually Owen got going on the phone. He was shocked to find that, with a little bit of encouragement, people would talk about themselves throughout an entire conversation. And much to Owen's surprise, they would also ask him about himself. The conversation easily flowed toward real estate without being forced. Over the next couple of years, Owen's time distribution switched to about 20 hours a week dealing with investors and 30 hours a week working his Sphere of Influence. Now he is working 20 to 30 hours less per week than he used to, and his income went from about $100,000 to $365,000 a year. Owen thanks me profusely for his progress and success every time we meet.

Today, five years later, Owen is completely work-optional and making well over $500,000 per year. If he chose to, he could stop working today and live a comfortable life on his investment properties and referral-based income, which he could hand off to his team for additional income.

For Owen, it was simple, and it only took expanding his comfort level in one category.

You're thinking: 'Will Owen's success work for me?'

Well, what if you expand your business in several categories where you currently feel uncomfortable, where you've seen other REALTORS® succeed?

How to Move Beyond What's Holding You Back

Like most of us, you have people you look up to, or perhaps just people whose success you envy. Pick a specific person you admire or envy. Observe their business. Look specifically for things they're doing that you would never do or have not tried. It's quite probable those people achieved the success you wish you had by doing that uncomfortable thing you haven't done yet. They could even use a business plan similar to yours, but they have a different mindset, more confidence, longer workdays, right?

So, what's holding you back?

What's preventing you from getting to where they are?

It may not be one specific thing they are doing. There are many different pathways to success. But it is likely something you are not doing.

What's limiting you? Think of successful REALTORS® in your office or industry who have taken a different road to success. For example, some might specialize in purchasing leads or knocking on doors, while you have built your business through working your SOI (Sphere of Influence) and picking up leads from open houses and client calls.

Using them as an example, write down a list of things they are doing to gain new clients that you have never done, or at least have never done consistently, such as:

- door-knocking
- cold-calling
- farming
- For Sale by Owner calls
- expired calls
- purchasing leads
- working with referral groups, such as BNI (Business Network International)

These are all examples of things that somebody may have never tried out or succeeded with, yet they are making a living working with their Sphere of Influence and getting leads and referrals through their current listings.

Once you have compiled this list, pick two things that you are willing to try, even if they seem like something you would not enjoy, or that you cringe at the thought of doing. Put some time into researching how those techniques have been used by others, write down your own plan for executing them, practice them for an hour or so before you begin using them, and then dedicate at least an hour a day to trying them out for a week or longer.

The reason you are doing this is not necessarily to greatly increase your income, although that can happen if you dedicate yourself to it. The best results will come because you're stepping out of your comfort zone and not because you are trying something new. It will come because of the effort and planning you put into something you didn't think you would be good at or didn't want to do.

Hopefully, you will now see you have been stuck in your business because you have been limiting yourself and, like most people, you have been unwilling to get out of your comfort zone, get out of the rut you've fallen into, and try new things to increase your income.

Conclusion

Up to now, you have likely found at least some level of success by working specific techniques and systems to generate leads. Whether or not this has brought you a steady, acceptable income, you may be stuck in a rut if you are not truly exceeding your goals and expanding every year. In order to reach the next level in your career, you must try something new. If you can fully commit to doing things uncomfortable and difficult for you, you'll be able to reach new heights in your career.

You may find this difficult to do. That is why in the following chapters we'll explore how you look at yourself, and why the way you look at yourself has caused you to put self-limiting beliefs and obstacles in your own path.

Chapter 2

Overcoming Your Limiting Beliefs

In this chapter, we will help you believe in yourself, which is essential to expanding your limits and realizing your true potential. You can learn to push yourself so you can move ahead — it doesn't take more than one strong action to have enormous results.

We will start with a story about an agent who learned how to push himself out of his comfort zone and succeeded tremendously. Then we'll discuss a few steps to thinking bigger.

Breaking into New Markets

A real estate agent named Bill was trying to break into a new market after moving to a new place an hour away from his old city. He was feeling frustrated. His self-limiting belief was that this new market was too hard to break into because he didn't have any contacts there.

As a result, for several years Bill actually traveled daily for an hour each way to his old market area to knock on doors and work with past clients. Bill would even cold-call there in his old market rather than in his new one. Bill believed this was justified because he had succeeded there and was making a good living, earning $250,000 a year. The downside was spending a lot of time driving and missing out on life and opportunity where he had moved to.

Finally, he came in and sat down with a coach. His coach had been trying for the longest time to get him to try something new. The town he had moved to, La Jolla, was a hard market to break into. Tiring of his daily commute, finally, he said to the coach, "I'm ready to try something new."
His coach asked him about his hobbies and what he liked to do in his off hours. Bill was confused about this question, but he discussed how much he enjoyed sports. As he was talking, his coach searched online for opportunities with local schools. "Here we go," she said to him. "I'd like you to go coach the high school football team. There's an opening for an assistant coach."

Bill was a little taken aback by the idea and asked why. "How do I have time to coach a silly high school football team if my whole purpose is to work harder on real estate, not picking up new hobbies that will waste my time?" His coach asked him to trust her and explained this would be an opportunity to get to know families in the area and to get people to know him. "La Jolla is about who you know," she said, "not about how many doors you knock on."

He agreed to coach the team. Over the next several months, he and his business coach started putting together a plan to use this opportunity to break into the local La Jolla real estate market.

Among the ideas they came up with was sending out a monthly letter to all the parents of the players. He made it fun, with items such as comparing football to life, and how someone's son could use his football experiences somewhere else. The letter carried life lessons, home tips, and each one included a picture of Bill with the players on the football team.

At least once a year, Bill would hold a party celebrating the team's success. He would always make it a nice catered affair, sponsored by his real estate company. Steadily, Bill built strong

relationships with many of the parents and, as was appropriate, began more personal interactions, such as taking some couples to dinner, along with their son or sons, of course. Eventually, Bill started selling to all the parents of the kids on the team. Football teams are pretty big, so he started adding thirty to forty more people into his database every year. His opportunities expanded even more wildly as the players grew up and started buying houses of their own, in La Jolla and nearby.
Eventually, Bill became one of the top-selling agents in La Jolla. He is now making over $1 million a year.

After initially resisting his coach's suggestions of trying something new and doing something he was uncomfortable with, all it took was Bill fully embracing that one new idea to propel his career to new heights. This is the power of having a little bit of courage and stepping into something you are uncomfortable with.

Three Levels of Success

Through the years, I've identified three levels of success in real estate. Bill was in the second level.

I've observed that most agents will get to one of these levels fairly naturally through their skill level or their work ethic. But once they settle into a level and become comfortable in it, then it becomes extremely hard for them to advance to the next level.

Below, I will take you through these levels, and then I will give you some to-do list items to help you break through and start working your way toward the next level.

Success Level 1

On this level, people accomplish almost nothing. But they have sold enough houses to hang on working as REALTORS®, even if it does not make sense for them to continue in real estate work.

Over the course of my career, I've even coached some at this level out of the industry. At the end of the day, they were unwilling to make the necessary changes to earn more than a bare bones living in real estate. When their income was based on sales, they were so limited they could not even get themselves to do a full day's work. For this reason, I advised them to get a 9-to-5 job.
Don't let this discourage you. I have helped many agents at this level get to a higher level within their agency. I just want to impress upon you the importance of breaking out of Level 1 right now. Level 1 agents are part of the 80% who end up quitting within the first several years of their real estate career.

Tips

Here are some tips to help you become part of the 20% that stays in real estate and advances:

Get focused NOW. If you are selling fewer than six houses a year, or a house every other month, stop what you are doing right now. Aside from essential tasks required of you by your current clients, spend the next several days working with a mentor or your broker and compare your daily activities with those of the successful agents in your office. This includes not only what time you start work in the morning, but what time you wake up, when you arrive at the office, what your activities are at the office, when you go home, and what you do once you are home.

You may not always have the ability to completely replicate these successful agents, especially if you have responsibilities within your home that prevent you from getting to work as early as they do. But there's one thing I've found when you are determined to have success — you can always find time to generate better results, even if you have to change your environment.

For example, early on in my career, my wife had many health issues. As I grew frustrated trying to fight my way out of Level

1, I discovered that successful agents in my office started work at 8 a.m. and would leave ten, eleven, or twelve hours later. Meanwhile, I was sitting on my couch at home at 10 a.m. with kids climbing over me while my wife was suffering in bed from her illness. I had a victim mentality. I would do a little bit of cleaning around the house, read a few real estate articles, and then spend hours on Facebook "cultivating relationships." When I was finally able to recognize my victim mentality, I began to build my business through reaching out via text messages to my Sphere of Influence and making cold calls while hiding in my pantry at home. I'll never forget pressing the "mute" button in-between every sentence I spoke so that people were less likely to hear my kids in the background. The really interesting thing was that on some of those cold calls, doing this would humanize me. Rather than being called by somebody sitting in a cubicle, they had me laughing and apologizing for my crazy kids. "Sorry, I'm working from home today," or, "My wife is sick and I'm working from home, sorry." All of a sudden I was not just a salesperson, but a human being with a family like theirs, and my kids were driving me nuts just like theirs did.

I could go on about the little tricks I did to sneak work in here and there, such as waking up three hours earlier than normal once in a while. But you get the point. I had to start replicating the hours and activities of my successful colleagues, and to do that I had to stop making excuses and get creative. You can do this, too.

Now that you've found a way to start being more effective and hopefully get a few more hours of focused work in every day, you'll find in the following chapters the importance of tracking numbers. Make sure you read those chapters quickly and start implementing the techniques to stay productive and focused during the hours you are working.

Get an accountability partner. Your broker, or a hired mentor, is a great resource as you try to make this big shift in your career. Make sure they know that you want them to be aggressive with you. You don't need to hear from them that you are trying your best, or that you'll do better next week. You need someone asking you if you hit your numbers and, if you did not, to ask you why. Sometimes it's good to have two accountability partners, perhaps another person who is trying to break out of Level 1, as well. You can keep each other motivated throughout the day, and then you can check in with a mentor every morning or evening to report your progress.

Success Level 2

Level 2, the next Level of Success, is made up of people who live month-to-month on a paycheck and survive by instinct. They are so laser-focused on the minimum amount of money they need to make to survive that they either barely reach it every month, or, when they reach it, they stop pushing in the following month and lose momentum.

Level 2 has a wider range of real estate agents than Level 1. Some Level 2 agents run out of money at the end of each commission cycle and are desperately waiting for their next check to be cut. But some are doing a bit better and perhaps putting away a little bit of money each month. In either of these cases, neither one is going to retire within the next 30 years. And both are probably frustrated about how tightly they need to budget their money, or how often they need to postpone vacations.

If you've recently thought some of these phrases, it's an indicator that you are in this category:

- "As soon as I get my next closing, I'll be able to ________________ (fill in the blank);"
- "We can go on that vacation this summer if I can close on a couple more houses before the end of April;"
- "I can't believe that deal just cancelled; how am I going to cover my mortgage now?"

Or perhaps you have promised your spouse that as soon as things pick up they will be able to buy that furniture they've always wanted. If any of these sound like something you have said recently, here are some tips to start breaking out:

- Immediately stop thinking about how much money you need to make to pay your bills. The reason you are frustrated today is because that's all you ever do. Making a goal based on this or even just having this number in your mind naturally limits your success to that number. It's time to create a new goal.

- Take all of your monthly expenses you are currently thinking about and add them up, including mortgage, car payments, utilities, etc. Now add to that list a weekly date night at the most expensive restaurant in your area. Perhaps it is $200 a week. Also add to that list enough to save up for several extremely fun vacations for a year. This could be an additional $2,000 or $3,000 a month. Also add enough that you are saving and contributing to your mutual funds or investment properties, at a rate that is extremely pleasing to you, and add enough that you're saving up for those luxury items you always wanted, and add enough so that you're saving for a rainy day. Is there anything else you wish you had money to put away for every month? A new car? Add that in as well. If you are like most people, your monthly budget probably just tripled. This is the new number you will have in your mind while you are setting goals, while you are "trying to earn enough to get by."

- Use the techniques in the following chapters to track your goals and to make sure you are holding yourself accountable. This will be covered in more detail later, but it's probably good at this point to create a vision board so that you can start focusing on positive things, rather than the totally negative influence of worrying about just paying your bills each month.

Success Level 3.

People who are in the third level of success have self-limiting beliefs of a different sort, and what may seem like a "luxury problem" to people in the first two levels.

REALTORS® who are making $350,000-plus a year might still have limiting beliefs that prevent them from fully enjoying life. For instance, they might shrivel up if you ask them to speak on stage. They are successful in many ways, but hold back in others. Public speaking is not the only example. Some of them are afraid to be mentors or teachers, or scared of public recognition, or any number of other fears.

If you are in this category of making several hundred thousand dollars a year, you may not even realize that you are stuck. Some of the key indicators of this are if you find yourself restless or unsatisfied on a daily basis with your work activities. Obviously, money is not as much of an issue for you as it is for the struggling REALTORS® in your office. But for some reason you do not feel totally happy with your situation. Perhaps you are looking forward to when you can stop being a REALTOR®, or you are growing tired of the process. **At this point, you are ready to advance beyond Level 3.**

It is not necessarily about money, but about fulfillment, and truly enjoying your career. It's worth noting, however, that as you break out beyond this level, you may very well make much more money than you are currently making.

- It's time to think bigger. A friend of mine who struggled through the first two levels for years and years finally reached Level 3, and he became infuriated with his wife one evening as they were sitting in front of the fire in their brand new 7,000 square-foot house. She asked him, "So, what are you going to do with yourself now?" He was angry and frustrated because he felt that he had finally 'made it.' But his wife knew better. So in that spirit, ask yourself that same question: What are you going to do with yourself now? What is important to you, now that you have plenty of money and perhaps even work fewer hours per day and per month than you ever have before? Take a few minutes to think about what you want to do in-between retirement and death.

- Hopefully, your answer was not, "Sitting on the beach and watching the ocean for twelve hours a day." If you are going to achieve a higher level of exciting success, you need to have a bigger reason why to do it. Do some brainstorming about some real change you could help create in the world. Is there a charitable cause or something else that inspires you? Would creating work opportunities for others bring you joy?

- In upcoming chapters, we will help you discover your big 'What-Why,' but now is a good time to start thinking this way. If you could double or triple your income, would you be willing to make a few changes, or perhaps what if you could create a work life that you were actually excited to wake up in the morning to get to?

If you're in Success Level 1 – those who accomplish almost nothing in real estate sales and merely hang on to their

REALTOR® jobs – you have to start writing down your reactions and decision-making process. At an almost rudimentary level throughout the day, when you react to something, write it down. If you wake up late, what is your thought? If you're getting ready for work, what's your thought? What if someone says they are not interested in buying what you're selling, what's your immediate thought? If you're not having any success, it's because of your mindset. When something bad happens, write down the first thought you have. You don't realize how negative you are unless it's written down, and you see it.
Some people I've worked with who've done this have been shocked at how negative they are.

The next step is to keep writing your reactions down, but do the opposite of your negatives: If you receive a call saying the caller isn't interested, instead of saying to yourself, "It's going to be a bad day," instead of writing something like, "This is why I never get ahead," write instead, "Because of situations like this, I'm going to work especially hard to get ahead. I won't worry about situations like this. I'll just work even harder to get ahead."

If you're in Success Level 2 – those who live month-to-month on a paycheck and survive mainly by instinct – you need to start challenging yourself. When you're presented with something uncomfortable, you need to actively attempt to do it. Here are a couple of examples.

Maybe you're at sales training, and they say you need to make X amount of phone calls a day, and your immediate thought is, "I hate cold-calling. My goal is to succeed by using other methods." To follow this program, you need to try cold-calling for a week. Make twenty cold calls a day for a week. Not because you're going to sell a house from this or get a ton of sales, but because you are training yourself to do something hard, so that when the next opportunity arrives you are not going to shoot it down because you're uncomfortable. You may even find you're good at the thing you don't like doing.

Another example: Maybe at a sales conference you are told

small get-togethers are a way to improve your Sphere of Influence and build better relationships. You tell yourself, "I hate parties" or "It's uncomfortable for me to have people in my house." It's probably not going to be as hard as you thought it would be. You might find it's actually something you are okay with.

People in the top level – Success Level 3 people, the super-successful but still with self-limiting beliefs – need to figure out a bigger What-Why and explore bigger goals.
I like to have REALTORS® close their eyes and imagine they have $100 million. You're all set up with investments. You live in your dream home. You drive the car you love. The day is yours. Why do you get up in the morning? Are you up at that point in your day, are you going to just walk around all day? What is your reason for existing at that point? What's going to bring you joy? It might not be doing some grand thing. Maybe you like vacationing with your kids and wife, or donating to charities. But the goal is to explore what you would do if money were no obstacle.

Even beyond that, if you had relatively unlimited money, are there charities that you are passionate about that you could contribute to? Or now that you have more time, would you be more active in them? Everybody I've asked this has had a surprising answer.

In doing all of this, you should see that you actually can succeed where you previously believed that would never happen because it was beyond your abilities.

Recap

Your current mindset that has gotten you to where you are – thinking of things the same way, doing things the same way, getting into a rut so deep you can't get out, no matter what – will not get you to a different place than where you are now. You need to start thinking bigger, sooner, more often, fresher, newer – start doing things you previously weren't willing to do in order to achieve the results you had thought were beyond your reach. Albert Einstein said it best: "We can't solve problems using the same kind of thinking we used when we created them."

Chapter 3

The Root of the Problem

Hopefully, now your mindset is healthier than when you started this journey. If you have completed the previous exercises, you're in the perfect state of mind to create visualizations for your future that excite and motivate you.

We will identify long-term goals that you may never have realized you had, and we will create a clear pathway for you to reach those goals in a reasonable amount of time. You are going to make your daydreams a reality and set the stage for future goal setting. The big idea is that creating detailed long-term goals and matching those goals with visualizations and strong feelings can push you to do things and work harder than you would normally be willing to try.

Visualizing Your Successful Future

It's a good idea to create one-, three-, and five-year visualizations. First of all, when you go through the process of determining your one-, three- and five-year visions, you are also figuring out your big What-Why : What it is you do and why you do it.

Your big What-Why becomes really significant after the first year and the first three years of your working life. That's when you need to decide what you really want to do, once money isn't a problem, or if you have so much of it that you need a greater purpose to get up in the morning.

We will start with a five-year vision, because it's important to start thinking big, way beyond what you might casually expect. And for those who have already achieved great success, you need to see what's next and why you should keep pushing. We should also look five years ahead because almost every aspect of your life can change within five years. So you should visualize a dramatic change for yourself five years down the road.

Now, you need to push yourself to think BIG . Just assume that you're making much more than you are now. If you say that in five years you'll be closer to paying off your thirty-year mortgage, then it's obvious your mindset is not in the right place. The goal is to get you way beyond that limited sort of thinking.

You can see this when people's big What-Why is still limiting, such as, "I want to retire" or "I want to travel." We need to dig deeper. When you finally realize what your big What-Why is, you will realize what you really want. Then we can help you create steps to get you there.

You will record your visualized goals on a piece of paper or another permanent document, so you do not lose them. This will help you focus.

Before you start this visualization process, it is important that you recognize that anything can change in five years. I've personally known many REALTORS® who have gone from making very little to over $1 million a year by the end of five years. Think of the next five years in that context.

Now, close your eyes and imagine that you are waking up five years from today. What does your room look like when you open your eyes? Is it a different house? What do the furnishings in your room look like? What size is your TV? Are you lying next to someone you love? You look over at your alarm clock. What time is it? What are your next steps today? Do you quickly head off to the gym? Do you shower immediately? Read? Meditate?

As you go through these steps, imagine your surroundings. For instance, in my visualization, before breakfast I would head down to my home gym. I imagine it would be five times its current size, with all-glass walls on one side, leading into an indoor basketball court. I would spend 30 minutes on the bike, 30 minutes on the treadmill, and then I would shoot baskets. I imagine every detail of this indoor gym, down to the decoration, which includes autographed jerseys from my favorite players, to the lighting and size of the gym itself.

Continuing through your day, as you go and eat breakfast, what does your kitchen look like? Who's there with you? And just as important, how do you feel as you perform these activities? Is there a sense of accomplishment as you walk through your dream home? Are you in a rush or can you take your time with your children as you laugh and joke while eating a bowl of cereal? In your ultimate reality, how do you feel about yourself during this entire morning?

If you are still working, what time is it now, as you decide whether you should head to the office? Or is it a home office? If you are going to the office, do you have your choice of car to drive? What kind of car do you take? Perhaps it's that Lexus or Tesla you've always dreamed of. As you leave your house and drive through your neighborhood, visualize what your house looks like from the outside, what your neighborhood looks like. How do you feel as you drive in this car that you've always wanted?

What city do you live in now? What do you see in your car window as you drive? Perhaps you pass your financial institution. Does it bring you a sense of comfort when you remember how much money is in your bank accounts there? What is that number? How much is in your savings/how much in checking?

Now you're passing a billboard about saving for retirement. This brings you comfort, because you now have X amount of dollars in your retirement investments. And you have X amount of rental properties. When you pull up to your office, I want you to imagine what the building looks like, what the environment looks like, and what your personal office space looks like.
It's time to dig into your daily activities now. Are you managing a team? Are you still doing sales yourself, or are you some kind of a leader or broker?

Remember to think a good deal beyond your current work restrictions. This is 1,800+ days from today. Imagine all of the things you could have changed about your career to this point. When lunchtime hits, are you going to a fancy restaurant? Who's going with you? What's the atmosphere like?

After you are done with work, what time do you decide to head home? Do you still enjoy working late? Or are you heading home at 3 or 4 p.m. to spend time with your family?

Obviously, this will change dramatically from person to person. Perhaps you head straight out to entertainment with your single friends, visiting local hotspots, movies, clubs, etc. What do these places look like? What is the atmosphere? How are you dressed? What are your interactions like with the people you now care about? In my case, I head back to my house and family, I watch movies in our custom theater, and I squeeze in an extra workout before heading out on a date night with my wife, after the kids are settled down.

And now, what time are you going to sleep? Your eyes are closed again. How do you feel about your day and your life?

After you have completed this task, do the same thing for three years from now. This is a perfect opportunity for you to get a framework for what point you need to be at in three years in order to get to your five-year goal.

For example, if now you have zero dollars, and the five-year visualization would require you to have $2 million dollars and $300,000 a year, three years from now you would need to have $700,000 in net worth and need to make at least $250,000 a year. Go through the same long process and complete your three-year visualization.
Once that is completed and there's a clear pathway from three to five years, do the same thing with one year from today.

Once you have completed this entire process for five, three, and one years, you will know exactly what you need to do for the next twelve months to be on track to hit your ultimate goal in five years. You are now in a position to create rewritten goals and to put in place systems to track your numbers so you can get to where you need to be at the end of the year.

There's a big difference between what you will do and what a lot of other people would do. Most REALTORS® would think, "So, I'd love to have a house on the beach, someday; I wish I had that nice car that Bob two doors down has. To have those things I need $100,000 a year. That's my goal. And maybe in 10 or 20, at the most, I could get a beach house, or in 10 that sports car, if I could just make $100,000 a year."

The problem is, whether they reach their goal or not, there's no clear map toward their ultimate destination. They are completely assuming what it will take to get to where they want to go. And not having a clear plan to get to the ultimate goal makes the one year goal less exciting and less important. Because, after all, if you don't do it this year, you can do it next year, right? With our plan, that is absolutely *wrong*, because you need every single one of these five years in order to reach your five-year goal.

So have your mentor help guide the session for setting your goals and visualizing, for that exact reason (many five-year plans are far from being real visualizations of the future, but more what life might look like if you achieve your minimum goals). Mentors are great in helping you not only to be granular, but also in helping you to see past your present situation.

Work backward from five years in the future. Don't think small. Don't think in terms of your current situation. Think in terms of your future expansion and freedom.
Not everything can change in one year. Most people have self-limiting beliefs, and, for many, three years is also too soon for real change. Five years is easier for most people to wrap their head around major improvements or successes.

Be concrete; be specific. Don't say to yourself, "Travel," if that's your five-year goal. A better example might be, "I will be working three days a week, mainly from home. I will be earning $1 million a year. I will have a team of people reporting to me. I will be delegating rather than directly involved in selling. This will give me plenty of time to travel throughout Europe with my family and live a flexible lifestyle. And I will also create a foundation to give back to charities to end human trafficking or perhaps contribute to cancer research." Be specific.

During the diagnostic interview process, I asked one client what would stop him from getting to where he wanted to go. "I don't believe in myself. I've never really succeeded," he said. "My friends succeed. But I do not."

I asked him how he defined success, and why he compared himself to others.

We dug down and learned that his parents used damaging language to him when he grew up, such as, "This is why you're never going to succeed," and "Why do you have to be so stupid? Why can't you be smart like your brother?" I got him into the habit of using positive affirmations to change his mindset. These included phrases such as "I am going to be successful because of ______ and ______," or, "Because I am intelligent and hardworking, I am reaching high levels of success."

We also found a few specific moments where he felt less successful, such as when he found out that his two best friends growing up were each making low six-figure salaries, nearly four times as much money as he was earning. It was even more difficult because one of them was a real estate agent. We talked about this friend, and I helped him realize that he could do the same things his friend was doing, and that he had the ability to make even more money with the proper plan and mindset.

Right now, he's doing really well. He's on pace to make over $100,000 for the first time in his life. He has distanced himself from the negatives in his life, mostly through practicing his new, positive mindset and his positive self-affirmations. Perhaps most difficult, he has stopped associating with and giving power to people who had a negative influence on his life. He can't completely distance himself from his own mother, for example, but he has created boundaries and stopped giving her power over his emotions.

You can do all this, too.

The Origin Story

Before I had developed this system, I stumbled into doing a five-year visualization completely accidentally.

At my local BNI[1] group, there was a financial advisor who had unique systems for helping people create a financial roadmap, as he called them. I wanted to invest in one of his products, but he would not allow it unless my wife and I came in for a consultation. This was incredibly frustrating for me because my wife didn't like being involved in finances, and talking her into sitting through a financial consultation literally took me more than six months to accomplish. He stood firm and required us both to come. When we got there, he had us do a visualization exercise similar to what I just explained. His exercise, however, was completely based on finances and the freedom and peace it would give us.

[1] Business Network International (BNI) is a franchised networking organization with more than 254,206 members in 8,968+ local chapters worldwide. Members in local chapters meet weekly to discuss business, and they support each other's businesses by sharing referrals.

He asked us where we wanted to be five years from that day financially, and he pushed us to imagine big. After some encouragement to go beyond simple things such as paying off our car or having half of our mortgage paid off within five years (which at the time seemed to be just a big fantasy), we were able to visualize what at the time seemed way too unrealistic. Our hope was to have a rental property 100% paid off so that we could use it as a pay-it-forward rental, for helping any family that is hit with an overwhelming hard time, or perhaps for helping a battered woman who needs a hideaway escape, allowing them to live there long enough to get on their feet financially and psychologically.

We also visualized owning a brand new car, owning a 5,000-square-foot home, having a couple of kids, and owning at least one other rental property. He asked us how much I would be making per year five years from that day. I started out at around $80,000 and with some probing from him, I got up to $150,000, thinking that was completely ridiculous.

We left that meeting and did not revisit these goals except while daydreaming every now and then. We did not create step-by-step milestones, as I have asked you to do, but that does not change the fact that I burned that goal into my mind. Just the thought of accomplishing that lifestyle and the peace of mind it would bring us became a big, motivating factor that drove me.

About three years later, I was cleaning out my office and stumbled across the financial roadmap the financial adviser helped us build. I was shocked to find that we had not only reached every single one of the goals on that list, but we had exceeded many of them. We actually had acquired the paid off rental property, and two families were living in it. I owned several other rental properties. and we had the exact amount of kids we had planned on. It had been only three years, rather than five, but having a clear visualization of what I wanted drove me to get there as soon as possible.

I am certain that if I had done all of the exercises I have since put my many clients through, revisiting those goals every week and creating detailed goals and milestones, I would have gotten there within a year and a half to two years. Clearly, I wasn't thinking big enough. I have since redone my five-year visualization almost every year, not only because my vision for the future expands as I get over self-limiting obstacles, but also because things change and priorities change, putting greater possibilities firmly into my grasp.

Here's another example of someone who wasn't thinking big enough — when I sat down recently with Tiffany, a young real-estate agent I'd begun to work with, I asked her to visualize what her life would look like in five years. She told me that her goal was to have $10,000 in her checking account and $10,000 in savings. Another goal of hers was having her bathroom remodeled.

I told her that these goals in themselves were self-limiting. "Some people are making $1 million in real estate," I said. "Did you know that? Could that possibly be your goal, making $1 million a year?"

The thing was, Tiffany thought of her future simply in terms of her past needs. She still believed that $10,000 in her checking account was a great achievement. She still believed that she would have succeeded if she were able to have her bathroom remodeled. Once we got beyond her limiting herself to past ideas of "nice, a-little-above-average results," it was cool to see her break out of her shell. Tiffany finally admitted that she really wanted things she hadn't dared dream of having before.

She's now doing much better, having visualized her future in concrete ways, and planning step-by-step what she needs to do to get to those goals. Recently, Tiffany closed multiple transactions in one month, for the first time in her career. She also threw away the dream of remodeling her bathroom, and she and her husband built their dream house. She's on her way to thinking much bigger and more successful even than that, such as her goal to completely replace her husband's income so that he can either come and work with her or pursue a career that he would enjoy. She also has the goal of being able to go on a limitless-budget vacation once a quarter.

You will begin to realize that your past and your current situations and accomplishments have been shaping your future and causing you to have self-limiting goals. After doing the exercises, you are now reaching for things again that you had once thought were impossible.

Conclusion

The power of visualization is so essential to you reaching your potential. Why? Because without a clear destination, it is impossible to know what road to take and how fast to drive. We will be looking at visualization in much more detail later in this book.

Chapter 4

What Is Holding You Back?

Now that you have very lofty but attainable goals, let me ask you the question I always ask:

> *Can you pinpoint a handful of things that would prevent you from getting to your visualized goals? What are they?*

The hardest thing for most people to accept is that, whatever list they start forming in their mind, most likely it has a problem they are causing or a problem they could actually solve. The difference is, most people believe it is out of their control, because they are either thinking as a victim or as an entitled person.

But to reach maximum potential, you must take ownership of your situation and realize that much more is in your control than you previously believed. You can change almost anything about your life, and you can absolutely change everything about your mindset and attitude.

Behavioral Change

First, you must recognize that your behavior has been like a victim's behavior.

For example, if you are asked to teach a class or to speak at a seminar, you might consider saying no just because it's not your thing, or you're not great at doing that. You're good at applying principles to make money yourself, rather than teaching others. You may not realize that this is a form of being a victim, because you're assuming that you're not good enough or skilled enough at something.
While driving to work, most REALTORS® have seen a sign in a yard of an acquaintance in their neighborhood, indicating that they are working with another REALTOR®. Most REALTORS® will jump into victim mode, saying, "Why didn't they use me? Maybe I'm not good enough." They think like victims. Most REALTORS® generally don't react by thinking, "Shoot, I need to improve my system so I'm seeing my own signs more often."

My reaction used to be a victim's reaction, too. But more recently, when such a thing has happened, my reaction has been that I haven't been working that neighborhood as much as I should. I think of opportunities where I should be doing something different, or I think that the REALTOR'S® probably a strong acquaintance of the homeowner, and there's nothing I can do about it. You can let go of that.

Instead of just being negative, start taking a little notepad around with you, and each time you find yourself thinking like a victim, or each time you have a success or failure, write it down (or text yourself). Maybe you get a phone call on one of your listings. It might not result in a sale, but you got a call from your sign — that's a success. Your client calls and wonders why you haven't called and updated — that's a failure, because you're not having good communication with them. Maybe you send your client info or pictures on properties, and they want to see them in person later that week — that's a success.

Make journal entries about the problems and successes of your day. Where did you miss out? Where did you do well?

Create a daily gratitude list: What are you proud of doing today? At the end of the day, you could write that you're grateful for waking up on time or getting enough sleep. You can write that you can get into work, and you're grateful you have reliable transportation, that you're able to make it to work without problems. The gratitude list moves you away from being a victim, because you can see all the things that are going well for you.
Halfway through your workday, take a little inventory and see how comprehensive your gratitude list is. It should be quite full. Where have you worked to change your attitude to become more present, more thoughtful? Have you been able to take negative situations and find something positive? For example, if I've had no phone calls today, I tell myself I'm glad for no interruptions today because I can work on projects I've been putting off: I'm grateful for the time I have to work on my to-do list.

Visualization (wake up and dream big for a few minutes) —

- Positive affirmation
- Positive self-talk
- Positive goal-setting, with tracking numbers to get to those goals on a daily basis
- Written accountability, through a coach, partner, or yourself, at the end of each day

Affirmations

Download the ThinkUp app, which has 100 or so affirmations in different categories. You pick what you want, they save into one place, and you record your own voice saying the affirmations; and then after you're done, it adds music in the background, and you listen to your own affirmations. It's a meditative thing. There's something about hearing your own voice with music that makes it easier for you to believe it, instead of just thinking it or saying it aloud.

From Victim to Responsibility

When I asked Aaron the question of what would prevent him from getting to his goals, he referenced his relationship to his wife: "Things are always difficult with her in regard to work," he said. "She wants me to work less hours, but make more money. She continually guilts me about spending time on my career, and she expects way too much of me in the home." He said, "Other successful people I know never have to do the amount of cleaning and babysitting that I do."

He then went on, "Because of this, I never have enough time for my clients and to truly become a success. My time at home is spent trying to improve my marriage and keep up with neglected things around the house. This results in me not spending enough time with my kids." Do you sense entitlement in these phrases? He had somehow felt that he deserved a similar situation to others, despite his lack of knowledge about their actual situation or relationships.

"This causes me a lot of guilt," Aaron said, "which clouds my mind and makes it even harder to work and succeed."

If you can't tell already, the big villain in Aaron's story was his wife. But when you sit back and reflect on his story, the true villain is that Aaron thinks he is the victim of several great injustices, and that they are all out of his control.

Luckily, we were able to break down his situation. Afterwards, Aaron was able to have some very difficult but important conversations with his wife. For instance, his wife wasn't upset because he worked so much. She was upset because he put no effort into the romance of their marriage and that he always used the excuse of being busy with work. Simply getting into the habit of occasionally taking two minutes to write a note and leaving it for her to find was all it took for her to start feeling special again. When she began feeling special, she viewed him going to work as providing for her and the kids, rather than leaving her and neglecting her.

Everything Aaron had thought about the situation was skewed. He had entirely misunderstood his wife's behavior. It was hard for him to realize that his actions were causing her to behave the way she was behaving. After making some improvements in his life and changing his behavior, she became extremely supportive of his work. Aaron's relationship with her improved immensely, despite increasing his work hours by about 30%. And those hours were extremely productive because the guilt about his home life was completely gone.

We also identified selfish hobbies that were not truly essential for his happiness, but were preventing him from spending time with his kids. The fact is that he followed several bands and public figures during his "down time" at home. His kids would beg for his attention, but he would be glued to his phone sometimes for two or three hours, reading articles and listening to those public figures. His excuse was it was his only chance to escape all of the turmoil in his life. He never even realized how much time he was spending on this and how spending time with his kids would have had an even more calming effect on his mind.

And by recognizing ways that he was being a victim at work, Aaron also completely changed his career. He was blaming clients and coworkers for problems he, himself, could solve.

For example, Aaron would often have frustrated clients and did not know why. The victim in him said, "I work with a lot of grumpy people who don't appreciate my efforts." When Aaron went to have those difficult conversations with current and past clients similar to the one he had with his wife, he found out they were not grumpy at all. It was Aaron who was making minor mistakes that would lead to a transaction full of frustration and miscommunication.

With several small changes and by putting a little bit of extra effort and care into his clients, he saw the trust level expand exponentially, to the point that when difficult things happened, or he made mistakes in a transaction, Aaron's clients would actually jump to his defense rather than jump down his throat.

When I last spoke with Aaron, his home life had improved so much that he told me of a conversation he and his wife recently had. They both agreed that they have never been happier, and that their relationship and the romance in their life is even stronger than when they were dating. Workwise, he is making over $300,000 a year now (over twice as much as before), and he now loves going to work every morning.

The hope here is that you can come to realize you have control over almost everything in your life and business. If there is a problem, whether you are the root cause of it or not, you very often have the power to fix it.

Conclusion

The thoughts that occur in your head throughout the day as you encounter problems and approach solutions are often likely being affected by a victim mentality. Most people have been framing their problems this way their entire life, and they have observed others doing the same. It's going to be difficult, but it's time to start taking responsibility, not necessarily for the problems, but for the solutions. You have more control than you have ever realized. By shifting your mindset toward empowered thoughts and positive affirmations, incredible results will just naturally follow.

Chapter 5

You Don't Have to Stay a Victim

Now we're going to look at how you can change your mindset so you can begin changing your work methods. Although people can increase how many hours they work or improve their systems or hire a coach to be more productive, without fixing and improving the underlying or root problem of mindset, they will revert back to old habits and their old level of success. That's because their belief system and self-talk will eventually catch up with them and pull them down.

The negative ways we think of ourselves are not necessarily the way other people see us. But if we continue to look at ourselves and our lives in a negative manner, it will also affect how other people see us and react to us. For this reason, your positive attitude about yourself is not just an improvement to your own emotional health, but will even draw others to you and improve your relationships with others and with yourself.

Getting Out of a Hole

Jason, an agent I have worked with, told me that he had given up believing he could get out of the hole he found himself in.

He was afraid of taking on additional projects in order to move ahead, and wanted to settle with what he had, and remain unfulfilled.

Jason's problem was a little bit different than most people's problems. The hole I'm referring to is that his business was set up in a way that his customers didn't respect him, in large part because he had labeled himself as a discount REALTOR®. He had built himself an image that his clients perceived him a certain way, and it was beginning to wear down on him. Also, because of being expected to always give a discount, he had to continue working two side jobs, despite selling more houses than most agents.

He had decided that things were okay the way they were, since with three combined jobs, he was able to provide for his family and even put aside a little in savings. He figured that he would simply push through like this until someday he could retire.

After trudging along for several years, Jason's hunger for something more returned. His two side jobs were doing well enough, and he had hired people to work them. So now he had unlimited time for real estate. But the old problems of feeling a lack of respect from his clients, and also boredom with the process he had done so many times, put him back in that same rut of lack of motivation.

Jason approached me about helping him with a new idea of starting a team. He had always loved leadership roles, and the idea of training new agents was new and exciting. He just had to make it profitable and, just as important, he needed to start feeling respected by his clients, or he would not be able to respect himself as a team leader.

I worked closely with him to teach him how to show his value. For example, Jason was one of the most creative advertisers I ever met. But he was also extremely humble. I explained to him, and we role played a little, the difference between explaining the process to your client and being cocky.

He always felt that, if he explained to his clients all the techniques he used, it would come across as, "I am the best REALTOR® in the world because I do such and such." What he

did not realize was that his sellers were hungry to know more about the process. And when he did not explain to them what he was doing, they thought of him as lazy. They had no idea how hard he worked or how creative he got in order to sell their homes.
For instance, one client was shocked to learn that Jason used his drone to create a music video about their listing. He used a drone to do a video circling the house while playing fun music, and then he expanded out through the neighborhood and got shots of the sunset and the mountain range. He also decked himself out in a complete superhero outfit and made a parody video newscast about the superhero who had been spotted around that home that was for sale. He had done creative things like that on all his listings. But his updates to his clients were simply, "Yes, we're still advertising," without letting them know how original his advertising was on their behalf.

I also coached him to ask for a more reasonable commission. We created a plan together about different methods for showing his clients his advertising techniques and processes so they would get an idea of the massive amounts of work he was putting in for them.

In the end, the process of getting a higher commission proved shockingly simple, even to my experienced eyes. Jason had a listing appointment coming up, and I pressured him to ask for a 3% commission. He was extremely hesitant and fought hard, saying this was not the time to do that. Not only had he sold another house at half price several years earlier for these clients, but these clients had referred him to other clients because of his discount.

I explained that he absolutely needed to charge a full commission on this sale, because if these people were referral partners they would continue to refer him to people who would expect the same discount. He showed them his new listing presentation with the added material we had come up with together, and told them the total cost would be 6% (3% for me and 3% for a buyer's agent).

They simply said, "Sounds great, we're excited to work with you again," and signed the papers. He called me immediately after this listing presentation, dumbfounded. We spoke a little about it, and I explained they must have been extremely impressed by his sales process. His next sentence has been repeated by many discount REALTORS® over the years: "I hate to think how much money I lost over the years by simply not asking for a fair commission." My response to him was, "Let's focus on how much more money you'll make in the future."

We continued to work on the difficult conversations that would be ahead with clients who might inevitably reference his past discounts. So he hired me to be a coach and mentor to the team we had talked about creating for him. Within just three months of the team being established and trained, they were the top-producing team in their brokerage.

Now Jason's the leader of a fully functioning team. He's charging a more reasonable commission, which has created a more respectful client base. He is donating a lot of money to charities he has admired over the years and spending more and more time as a philanthropist, supporting community projects, which has brought him a lot of joy and fulfillment.

Getting What You Need

So, here's a way to pump up yourself and your approach to work.

- Make sure your ThinkUp app is up and running, and that you are listening to it at least once in the morning and once before you go to sleep. This is important, because no matter how many times you write or think or say aloud an affirmation, there's something about hearing your own voice saying those affirmations that is extremely beneficial. Often, it creates a very positive emotional response, because you are who has been beating yourself down for 20, 30, or 50 years, and to all of a sudden hear your own voice switch course and build yourself up, it is jarring for most people, but in a good way. It's more convincing because you're the one who programs your mind; people might give you the material that hurts you, but it's your thoughts and constant beating down of yourself that makes that a core belief about yourself. You need to hear yourself give yourself permission to believe that you are worth it.

- Make a positive thought log for what you are doing each day, specifically detailing the self-limiting beliefs that are holding you back the most. The best way to do this is whenever you have a positive thought, write it down. And whenever you have a negative thought, replace it with a positive thought, say it out loud, and write it down. This is important because it will teach you how to catch yourself before you even have the negative thought, or at the very least how to correct it and replace it immediately with the positive thought. The reason you are saying things out loud, recording them and listening to them, and writing them down, is that you are trying to program your brain from different angles. By using this multiple-angle approach and excessive affirmation, you can undo years of damage in weeks.

- Sometimes it is really productive to select just one self-limiting belief or mindset that you'd like to switch to a positive. To do this, one successful method is to rate yourself at the end of the day on a scale of 1 to 10, one being that you continued to think that same self-limiting belief without any correction, and your day went poorly in regard to improvement. A ten would be if you did not think that limiting belief a single time, but, when the opportunity arose to think it, you thought a positive thought instead.

Most people will struggle to get past a 4 or 5 for the first several days, so do not get down on yourself. Remember, we are undoing years, and sometimes decades, of damage.

- A good place to record this and create a log would be in a journal. At the start of each entry, you will put your rating. For example, "January 15. 5 out of 10 for believing I am a likeable person." Now, create a journal entry describing your journey toward that rating. Write down the negative moments you will correct tomorrow and, most important, write down all your successes where you overcame that limiting belief and began to think positively. Keep the majority of your journal entries positive. Focus on your accomplishments and progress. Because it's almost impossible to track progress in any other way on changing your mindset, keeping a progress journal is very important.

With these techniques, you will become less of a victim and more of an achiever. Your negative self-talk and your negative programming will end, and it will be replaced with positive mental programming that will set you up for incredible success, and it will get you out of your own way in achieving your goals.

Conclusion

To recap, everybody has programmed themselves mentally in one way or another. Some do it in a very positive way, but most people's programming is primarily negative. If you're able to find and identify that negative programming, use these methods to stop it and replace it with positive programming, You will be able to rewire your brain and become more like those people you've always looked up to and wondered how they have achieved such a high level of success and how they can talk about themselves in such a positive way. We've all seen these people. They are confident and proud, but somehow they show it in a humble way.

Chapter 6

Becoming Empowered by Finding Your ' Big What-Why '

Here we're going to explore how you can think beyond your self-imposed limits and determine your ***big what-why***. In the previous chapter, we started the work to get you to break down your own walls that are self-limiting you, and to begin thinking beyond your self-imposed limits. Now that we've started to see success there, you should be in a better head space to discover what your ***big What-Why*** is.

No matter how successful you currently are, if you have not yet discovered your ***big what-why***, odds are you have not become fully empowered. For this reason, your full potential may still be out of your reach until you truly understand what your own unconscious goal is, your ***big what*** is, and exactly ***why*** you want to get there.

Finding a Bigger What-Why

Kevin had been a REALTOR® for about five years. Like just about every other REALTOR®, he was still trying to figure out how to gain leads through social media and how to interact with possible clients in the ever-changing digital world. In his sixth year of his real estate career, he finally felt he had cracked the code with social media and was beginning to gain a lot of leads through Facebook. He had also finally developed his skills in cold-calling to the point where he could sit on the phone for a single day and come away with several high-quality leads.

People would ask him all the time how he was able to do these things. And so he was offered a position at a brokerage teaching others how he does it. Part of his job description was to teach agents at least once a month about cold-calling and to train them in telephone and media skills.

Whenever Kevin did teach courses, he did very well when the class consisted of five or fewer REALTORS®. Even agents who had been in the industry for 10 or 20 years eagerly took notes and were amazed at his techniques. Kevin's teachings were seen as very valuable, and the way he presented it all made everything seem simple and replicable by any REALTOR®. Kevin was often offered opportunities to present his training to bigger groups of agents, some of them willing to pay him to do so.

But Kevin turned down paid speaking opportunities, because he had a very unreasonable self-limiting belief that a larger group of people would not appreciate his training and information as much as a smaller group.

While we discussed this self-limiting belief, Kevin would say things such as, "I can convince a group of three to five people when they get skeptical about my techniques. A group of 50 or 100 people might have several know-it-alls who boo me or ask questions trying to prove me wrong."

I pointed out to him that neither I nor he had ever been to a seminar where the speaker was booed by anybody. And while I had been to seminars where smart-alecks would ask questions trying to appear more knowledgeable than the speaker, I was positive that no one could poke holes in his presentation. Kevin's training was airtight. He had already addressed every possible objection from his smaller groups and overcome them easily. His methods were proven.

Eventually, Kevin was offered the opportunity to speak to an entire brokerage. The broker was trying to convince him to switch over to them, because she was so impressed with what agents said about working with Kevin one-on-one. It was implied that if he did well during this speech, he'd be offered a well-paid position with the company.

Kevin was terrified. "There could be 60+ agents there," he said when we spoke about it. We went over everything I had told him before about how airtight his presentation was. I helped him create three or four very helpful phrases and told him to write them down over the next two days, which was the amount of time he had to prepare for the presentation. I instructed him to say these phrases aloud as he drove around. I told him to say them with confidence, quietly and loudly, and with authority. I cautioned him that he might feel like a crazy person while doing this, but that was natural. Two of his phrases were, "When the pressure is on, I come alive" and "I perform best in front of large groups of people."

Luckily, I was able to attend that training of his at the brokerage, as they did not limit it to members of just that brokerage. Kevin presented for a full two hours, and he seemed to me to be completely confident and in control. He answered questions, and excitedly moved from topic to topic in an easy flow. After the seminar, he was ecstatic. Despite his years of beating himself down about public speaking, even Kevin was able to acknowledge how well it went. Now, Kevin presents in front of groups of similar size every week, sometimes multiple times in a single week. Not only is he not afraid to do so, he looks forward to it and even craves the opportunities for doing it.

Kevin was offered that good-paying job at the brokerage. But he turned it down for a quite similar position that offered him twice as much salary at another firm.

The Big What-Why of Affirmations

The reason Kevin had such a quick transformation was that he took action in addition to speaking his affirmations. When given the opportunity, if you can take on a challenge or try something that contradicts your negative self-talk, and approach it by practicing positive affirmations as Kevin did — ***do it***! Start today looking for such opportunities for yourself, while confidently continuing your daily affirmations.

So what is the point of expanding your career and tackling new opportunities? Many people who never truly put forth the effort simply don't know why they should do it. They don't have the motivation. What is the point of reaching these lofty goals, they ask themselves? This is especially true for people already making enough money to have a comfortable retirement, someday, at their current rate of success. For this reason, it is essential that you ask yourself right now: What is my ***big what-why***?

Your "***big what-why***." Hopefully, after doing your five-, three-, and one-year visualizations, you have created the blueprint for a potential life for yourself so that when you wake up every day you're not going to be wondering how to pay bills or how to get to the next month without running out of money. You can now answer the question of what you would do with your week or your month if you never had to think about money again. What would be your reason for continuing to get out of bed every morning at a reasonable hour? We find our big ***what-why*** by eliminating all the current reasons why you do what you do.

These current reasons are most often financial. So a simple exercise is to imagine you have $1 billion in your bank account today. Moving past the next several months — inevitably filled with fun vacations and partying, no doubt — what would be your point of living after the excitement of having so much money died down? What would you do with that kind of money? Hopefully, rather than buying a yacht and as many luxury vehicles as possible, you will recognize that true happiness comes with having a good purpose. So the real question is: If you not only did not need to worry about money but had an abundance of it, what change would you try to make in the world?

You should spend a lot of time pondering these questions. Think about it all when you lie in bed awake at night, or when your mind wanders and tries to visualize and dream of changes that you would like to make in the world. One example, lofty though it may be, is my hope to help the entire continent of Africa have a robust economy and a lifestyle similar to Americans. In fact, I've daydreamed so much about it, I have a strategy and budget in mind of what it would take. Talk about a ***big what-why***! The budget for the first phase of my plan would be about $100 million. (Pssst! If you know of any likely potential investors, please let me know! ***Seriously!***)

It is important to continue visualizing, daydreaming, and fleshing out your "***big what-why***." But in order to get there, you need a realistic pathway. For this reason, it is time to:

- Visualize your expected success continuously. It's important for you to visualize and give yourself permission to expect success beyond what you have now or beyond what you thought you would ever have. Until you are visualizing it continuously and looking forward to it persistently, you're never going to truly believe it and never do all that's needed to actually fulfill it.

- In order to get to that next level of success, another important technique is positive self-visualization. This is slightly different from positive affirmation in that you're elaborating, filling in the details. "I'm so glad that I overcame my self-limiting beliefs about public speaking, and now people love when I speak. It is incredibly fulfilling to see their eyes as they are inspired and learn from me. I'm so grateful that I have become an influencer and an inspiration to so many people." As you can see, positive self-visualization is more about telling yourself an unfolding story, having a conversation about the positive rather than just affirming it again and again. It's important that you also do positive talk about yourself with others. For example, if somebody were to ask Kevin if he liked speaking in public, he could easily say, "Yes, I really enjoy it. And I discovered that I have a gift for it." It is possible that you'll feel like a total liar and a fraud at first, but push through it. When someone asks, "What are your strengths?" it is okay to respond with something that you are aspiring or working towards, even if it is not currently a great strength in your own eyes. You are actually speaking it into existence.

Now you are eagerly looking for opportunities to do the things you are uncomfortable with, because you are now clear about exactly ***What*** you want to achieve in life. And that ***What*** has become your motivating ***Why*** for doing uncomfortable things. You will find that you are quite willing to do uncomfortable and even hard, difficult things and work harder than ever before in order to reach them.

So you should find a coach or an accountability partner willing to work with you and follow up with you to make sure you fully accept and follow through on all challenges that will help you fulfill your ***big What-Why.***

Conclusion

No matter how long and how many times you have told people that you're not good at something, it is possible not only to change your self-belief system about that, but it is also possible to become good at doing that thing.

You can do this in a much shorter time than you ever thought possible by practicing positive affirmations and positive visualizations. And when you do become skilled at things that previously had been seen as weaknesses, your future potential completely expands in a good way. You realize that things that other successful REALTORS® do, and have always seemed beyond your capability, are now fully within your reach, because you are completely, positively committed to fulfilling your *big What-Why*, your true motivation for tackling all your career challenges in real estate.

Chapter 7

How Your Mindset Affects Sales

Now let us explore how you can improve your selling by improving your sense of self.

Success in selling is built on confidence and belief in your product. Many times what people feel they are buying is *you*, as well as your real estate product. If you do not believe in your product and don't have confidence in yourself, why would anybody ever purchase what you are selling?

The human mind is incredible in its ability to believe what it chooses to believe. The events in your life have caused you to believe in certain negative things about yourself. We will now help you replace them with fictitious but realistic events that your mind will eventually convince you to accept and believe are true and empowering.

The Power of Self-Belief

When I was young and throughout my early career into my twenties, I really struggled with believing in myself. At times it still gets to me. If I could go back in time, I would raise myself with an extreme amount of encouragement and constant positive affirmations.

Unfortunately, in the 1980s and 1990s, there were no Facebook

memes and a lot less public material to remind my parents to be positive with me. In fact, I can probably count on one hand the number of times my father said something profoundly encouraging. On the other hand, I can remember many times he said something profoundly discouraging to me. My father's an amazing man, and he is actually one of my heroes, but that doesn't change the fact that my self-limiting mindset was strongly enforced by his words and actions.
For example, when our family would go bowling and I'd throw a gutter ball or get a low score, he would say in a kind of kidding way that he wasted money by taking me bowling. As for other sports, he was no less dismissive. He knew of my dream of playing in the NBA, and he knew the odds were quite low of my reaching the NBA. But rather than encouraging me to chase my dream, he said that would never happen and that I needed to give it up. The effect of all this has been to limit my self-confidence.

When I started to chase big dreams or have big goals, I would hold back because my brain had been programmed to never do that, or to give up because it was too hard, or to believe that too few people ever make it that big or achieve those types of dreams, and that I was certainly not one of them.

A big part of the positive change for me has been that I found a cheerleader, somebody who was always positive with me, even during my failures — my wife. Unfortunately, a lot of people's spouses are more like my dad, negative and merely 'realistic.' My wife, on the other hand, would say things like, "You're the smartest person I know, I believe in you." Over time, her positive, encouraging words and actions reprogrammed my brain.

I also found another mentor, Chris, who encouraged me to try a version of what I am sharing with you here. He helped me through the process of revisiting early memories, ones that usually imprint something positive or negative on the brain. He helped me pretend that my wife was actually there during certain childhood situations and to imagine what she would have told me if I had gone beyond my interaction with my father and went straight to her. He asked me to imagine what my wife would have said in response to what had just happened with my father. Chris encouraged me to close my eyes and put myself back in such negative moments with my dad, but then adding positive interactions with my wife at the end of each of them.

Honestly, it was quite emotional, reliving each of those events that were so damaging to me. I knew what my wife would have said, though: "He's so wrong. You can do whatever you want to do. I believe in you so much. Don't worry about it." She would have given me an encouraging rub on the top of my back and a little hug. Reinventing those events into positive experiences started me on a process where I could continue to do it on my own.

I could see that replacing all the negative events in my life with something encouraging might help me reprogram my brain a little bit quicker. So I took out a notepad, and I started writing down each and every negative event with my dad. Obviously, I did not want to spend 10 hours writing, and I would not want you to do that, either. So I wrote down short headlines that would remind me. For example, the story above would be, "Discouragement at the bowling alley."

After spending some time doing this, I was able to find 30 or 40 instances that reminded me a bit of the core memories in the Pixar movie, *Inside Out*. My core memories shaped a lot of who I was. So I went ahead and did the same exercise with each of those memories. More often than not, I started to replace my wife with myself, because I thought it was healthier to imagine that I was self-empowered during those moments. I went back and revisited each of those moments dozens of times, to the point in my mind now that I cannot discern the reality of what happened compared to the new version I created. I even started developing memories that included images of people's reactions to what I said in defending myself. The human brain is incredible. I truly feel I replaced moments of my life with a movie I created, and when I go back and try to recreate the original moment, the movie plays instead.

Here's how this has truly healed my mind. As recently as one year ago, I had an extremely negative interaction with someone I was beginning to trust and to consider a partnership with on a different joint venture.
After he blew up in anger for something that I totally did not understand and started to show his true colors, he sent me a text that read, "Building a coaching company is a mistake. Markets are heavily saturated…." Later on, we spoke on the phone, and he essentially told me that I would absolutely fail, along with some other hurtful and rude language about my capabilities and integrity.

For a moment, it shook me, mostly because I had gone in mere moments from trusting him to hearing all that negativity. But that only lasted about five seconds. My next thought was, 'Now I'm even more determined to succeed, and I wish I could be there to see his face someday when he sees how successful my coaching business is.' Since that moment, I have never worked harder to reach that exact goal of building my coaching company.

How to Overcome Self-Limiting Beliefs

This system has now worked not only for myself, but for several of my clients who had big problems breaking through self-limiting beliefs. It can work for you, too. Here's how to begin:

- Do what I did and start to search those incidents in the past that caused you to have self-limiting beliefs. Sometimes it is helpful to try to follow the belief and the feeling you have when you think about it, and try to search your memory for the last time you felt that feeling. This can sometimes trigger a memory better than sorting through random memories in your mind.

- Now that these circumstances are flowing into your mind, do what I did and write down a quick headline, and maybe a couple of quick notes that will remind you of the story later on. Try to find a minimum of 5 of these moments. Take a few days to do it. They don't need to be scarring, but just supporting moments that reinforce self-limiting beliefs. When you are taking these notes, be sure to write only one incident at the top of each page and leave the rest of the page blank.

- Now it is time to rewrite those stories. Take the first one on the list and close your eyes. Try to emotionally take yourself back to that moment and try to remember it in great detail. Now imagine you are back in your old circumstance, and the person is speaking directly to you in real time. After they are done speaking, write down the pertinent parts of the negative experience. And then provide a positive ending to that event. For example, you could go directly to one of your greatest cheerleaders, or you could stand up for yourself and walk away truly believing they were wrong, and you were right. Write down this positive reaction in detail on the rest of that page.

- Now that you have created a new version of the event, do the same for each of the events on your list. And relive each of them, preferably the first time with your eyes closed, so you can truly imagine you are in that moment. Now, as you do that throughout each day, naturally, recall those events in your life, except instead of remembering them as they were, remember them in the new way that you created. Try hard to imagine people's reactions, the faces they would make, and the feelings you would feel after being defended by someone else. You will eventually start to have a little bit of confusion as to which story was actually the true one, and hopefully, in the end, your mind will remember the positive outcome and the positive feelings it created.

- The future: Whatever this self-limiting belief or thing is that you're trying to overcome, now it has been completely cured, and when people tell you similar limiting things, then it's completely water off your back, and your reaction is, "Watch this," as in "Oh, really? You don't believe I can do it? Well, watch this." Creating a plan or visualizing how you will react to these situations in the future will make it more automatic and easier. It's similar to parents with kids with disabilities. They'll practice bullying in the home, that way the child immediately knows how they want to react when the bullying occurs. You should do the same thing now.

- Set up goals. This means, if your self-limiting belief was like mine, that when you are presented with a big dream or idea, rather than being fearful and negative, your goal is to be excited and positive.

- Make weekly written evaluations to track your progress, similar to the previous chapter. Rate yourself on a scale of one to ten. An interaction with someone who causes a self-limiting belief doesn't happen every day, so you might fill it out once a week, such as, 'This week, how did I react to new dreams and possibilities?' If you reacted poorly, as in you did not believe the new dreams were possible or you do not have the ability to accomplish the new possible opportunities, that would be a one or two out of ten. Obviously, if you were presented with new opportunities and took the bull by the horns and completely believed in your ability to reach/create goals, that would be a ten out of ten.

- Create deadlines. So you might decide, by the end of September I want to have a ten out of ten score two weeks in a row on this mindset I'm working on. It's important that if you get to the end of September and you're not at your goal, you absolutely must avoid beating yourself up, and adjust the goal for a month or two later.

You will be able to outsmart your own mind and rework the situations that caused your limiting beliefs to the point that you no longer believe them and, in some cases, question if they even happened the way that they did.

Conclusion

Some people in your life have denigrated you rather than cheered you on. Unfortunately, that's what usually happens with the majority of people. Even if it was not discouraging the majority of the time, psychologists say that you will remember negative things that were told to you more often than positive things, at a rate of ten to one. You can reach back in time and reprogram your brain from the beginning of the problem, rather than solely relying on current positive affirmations.

Chapter 8

Being a Victim Affects Your Sales

When you don't accept responsibility for who you are or move past what is holding you back, your relationships, your sales, and your career will suffer.

Most people, especially those who have attained mild success, may be surprised to hear or even be a bit offended to be referred to as a victim. But the fact is, there is probably not a person on earth who does not have some fears in their life that they feel they can't control, that they feel they can't do anything about — in other words, that they are victims of. Here we will figure out how to identify that victim mentality and overcome it.

Unaware of Victim Mentality

Some things I have heard from victims: "I'm bad at time management," "I can't try new methods," "I'm afraid of starting new projects or can't finish projects," "I'm unwilling to make cold calls, to approach people I don't know; and I'm bad at closing."

They say, "I'm not a salesperson," "I don't like being salesy," "I'm bad at parties," "I'm not a social person," "I don't want to knock on doors," "I don't have any contacts in the area," "People don't like me," "I just moved here and don't know anyone," "I'm not smart enough," "I don't have the time," "My spouse doesn't support me," "I don't believe in myself," "I don't want to be inauthentic," "I'm bad at presenting," " I don't want my friends to feel that I'm trying to sell them something or benefiting from them financially."

This is only a fraction of some of the things I have heard REALTORS® say, and they come across as excuses. Digging a little deeper, these are not only excuses, but excuses made from a victim's perspective. In their mind, all of these things are out of their control. These folks believe that they're victims of their circumstances or skill levels.

They're not aware that their victimization is a bigger problem than they realize. They blame their current lack of success on their company. This can come from entitlement, believing that their company should be creating success for them, or from victimization, believing their company is hurting them or favoring other people.

Brady G is someone who has been both a victim and entitled. His very first real estate transaction was with a friend. If Brady had had my sales process, it would have been fine, but he made mistakes, and he felt he had damaged his relationship with that friend. A few things happened that he had no control over, but because Brady didn't have a plan to communicate problems, he left his friend in the dark, and his friend believed that it was deliberate.

"You have known this for a week and a half," his friend said at one point to Brady. "Why didn't you tell me?" The truth was that Brady had no system for communication, so it didn't occur to him. Although the transaction went through, for both Brady and his friend/partner it was a bad experience. It created in Brady a fear of working with family and friends.

As I coached Brady, I realized that he had several other self-limiting beliefs. He felt that he wasn't smart enough and that his wife didn't support him, thus he didn't believe in himself. The biggest thing holding Brady back was what had happened with his friend, so he did not want to come off as salesy to friends and family. He did not want them to think he had ulterior motives or that he was trying to benefit from them financially.

The biggest thing preventing Brady from making a living in real estate was that not only was he unwilling to market to and work with friends and family as their REALTOR®, he also avoided them, to the point where his Sphere of Influence began to diminish.

Every now and then he'd stumble into a sale or pick up another lead from a REALTOR®, and sometimes his family would use him, but it was never enough to support his own family. As a result, he had to take part-time jobs, which he would eventually quit to do a full-time job before quitting that job and returning to real estate.

Unfortunately, Brady had a wealthy father, so he could fall back and work for his dad, even though he hated doing it with a passion. Brady eventually came to me for advice on how to stop this cycle.

It was clear that the first thing we needed to work on was overcoming his fear of making a living from working with his friends and family. It started with a simple question. I asked him, "If you had all the money you needed, all the time you needed, what would you do with your Sphere of Influence? What would your relationship be like?" He said, "I'd hang out with them more and we'd go to more parties. I'd go on vacations with some of my friends and their spouses. In reality, I would be a much better friend because I would not be as busy or stressed out about money."

I let silence hang in the air for a short moment and told him to think about what he had just told me. His eyes lit up when he realized what I was implying. The best way for a REALTOR® to win friends and family as clients is to hang out with them more, go with them to parties more often, take them on vacation, and be a much better friend.

As soon as Brady realized that being a REALTOR® was all about being a better friend, and actually helping friends have success during one of the most important transactions of their life, he was able to start marketing to them without feeling like a jerk. His new feeling was that he cared about these people. And because he cared about them, he wanted to be the one helping them with this difficult transaction, to make sure they were being taken care of and handled honestly.

One of the ways we started working on building up his reputation as a REALTOR® again was on Facebook. I helped him realize that it was okay to talk about his career on Facebook. He did not need to be pushy. He could simply write about how much fun he had showing houses on any particular day, or perhaps post funny pictures of things he saw while viewing houses and talking about how he loves his job.

Rather than endlessly scrolling through his Facebook page, he made it a goal to create true relationships. I had Brady click on specific people's profiles and scroll through their posts in an effort to try and get to know them better. Often, he would see things such as a trial they were going through, which would give him an opportunity to be there for them and to be a better friend.

It was no surprise that Brady started to see a huge increase in the number of friends and family who would randomly message him or call him and ask for advice on real estate. He even got a few of the famous calls we all look for when he picked up the phone and heard someone say, "Hey, could you list my house?" He finally had an opportunity to make a real living for his family, and to enjoy doing it.

Getting Past Negativity

Write down three daily thoughts that negatively affect you in one or more areas during your workday: Where do you hold yourself back? Rate them from most to least damaging: one, two, three.

With these thoughts, we are specifically looking for things that will stop you from getting to your goal. For example, your three thoughts could be: 1. I don't enjoy talking to people. 2. I'm always dropping the ball and disappointing clients. 3. I don't have anywhere to work; my home is a mess, and I can't afford office space, so I'll never be productive.

After you have written these down, come up with a few positive affirmations and positive visualizations for each item. Once you have done this, open up the ThinkUp app and create a separate playlist just for these three beliefs that are holding you back.

Every morning when you wake up, listen to that playlist on your phone at least once while you are still lying in bed. If you cannot do that, or if you wake up too late, listen to it on your way to work or perhaps when you're getting ready for the day. After you are done listening to the playlist, repeat it again, but alter it to fit the events of your day. For example, if my three things were the ones I just mentioned, I might say something like this: "I'm glad I enjoy talking to people, because I'm meeting with the Johnsons today. I know I will take good care of them because my clients are always satisfied with my process. I will continue to stay productive wherever I end up needing to work from." In this positive affirmation, you will notice I countered the victim attitude by addressing all three victim fears.

In fact, you will be building a routine for creating daily positive thought logs. Another example of something somebody might say to prepare for their day could be, "I'm super excited for my listing appointment. My presentation will be powerful. I'm going to be relaxed and win the listing. It's awesome that I have that training at 12 o'clock. I'm going to learn enough that it's worth my time ten times over. It will really boost my career." Don't be afraid to continue saying these things over and over again until your first appointment. You can even write them down.

Continue to use the ThinkUp app as a daily motivational tool. Now that you have created a playlist of affirmations, think about other aspects of your life that will be helpful for your playlist. For example, I have a separate playlist for weightlifting and playing basketball. Some of the phrases in my basketball playlist are, "I always have energy," "I am the best shooter and I make every shot I take," and "I am an incredible athlete." Don't be afraid to be a little bit cocky with these. Remember, you are the only one who will ever hear them, and you are trying to build yourself up so that you truly believe these things and so you can perform them without mental obstacles or reservations.

Eventually, you won't allow external forces to control your thoughts. Through the use of affirmations and the ThinkUp app, you'll be able to control your mindset in advance, and as a result, you will overcome self-limiting beliefs that would have damaged your productivity that day, or avoid them altogether and reach your goals, which will increase your sales.

Conclusion

When you observe your thoughts, reactions, and consequences, and specifically look for instances when your mindset is that of a victim, you, like most people, may be surprised to find that you do often have that mentality. As you identify these specific thoughts and work on a plan to overcome them, the results that you obtain will be pleasantly surprising and potentially even life altering.

Chapter 9

How You Can Overcome Yourself and Increase Your Sales

All of the positive visualizations and positive affirmations we have spoken of will certainly help your career, but they will not get you to your ultimate destination without a game plan and a way to track progress in your business. Here, we will begin to lay the groundwork for having an amazing business plan and tracking your numbers supporting that plan.

By visualizing your future, using tools such as goal-setting, accountability, positive affirmations, and creating a master to-do list, you can increase your sales and build your business.

Overcoming Lack of Focus

Let me share a story with you about how positive affirmations and focus helped a REALTOR® I worked with. Taylor had been a REALTOR® for about three months. He found himself hitting the wall daily after he completed one or two tasks.

His problem was focus. He attended many real estate seminars, read many articles and several books on how to be a real estate agent, and, although he was very dedicated to doing what was necessary, the information gathering in his head was taking up too much room. Taylor had too many things he wanted to do without having an organized plan for using them together.

As a result, when he would remember that he needed to do a certain task, he would do what he could in that category and then immediately move onto something else, without a plan. For example, he might remember something he had read in a book about the need to go knock on doors to build business. He would do that, then go home and remember that he had to do some social-media posts, and then he'd do that. It became overwhelming, this unrelated succession of tasks he would randomly remember that he should do.

So, Taylor would freeze and not know what to do next, because he wasn't getting results from those things he did when he randomly remembered to do them. When I began to coach him, I helped Taylor create a master to-do list, and took everything that was muddling up his brain and put it all down on paper.

The goal of doing this is to clear your mind. Once something is put down on paper, you can stop worrying about it and focus more on individual tasks. Once we did that, we prioritized and categorized the tasks, working on one item at a time until it was fully completed, and then moved onto the next one. By the time we were done that day, the to-do list had almost 70 organized items on it.

Every week when we would do those calls and I would hold him accountable, we'd have a schedule of everything to do between one call and the next one. He went from selling one house in his first three months — a partnered deal that he didn't generate — to making over $100,000 over the next nine months, while holding a full-time job as a computer programmer. That convinced him to transition full-time to real estate, with the goal of making $250,000 a year, a goal he actually accomplished in about eighteen months.

We set up a business plan, so he will never run out of things to do. Normally, he'd do one or two things then twiddle his thumbs. But now he had everything laid out for the year. While working full-time as a computer programmer, he was able to surpass his previous combined income within the first year of being a full-time REALTOR®.

How to Find Focus

Create a vision. Creating a clear vision is imagining a perfect week, imagining being completely productive, and reaching your goals every single week. That's what it would feel like every Sunday when completing another week's work, progressing toward your goals, and overachieving on a weekly basis.

Set up goals. This is where you need to start using flash reports. A flash report is a document you use to track numbers. If you reach your numbers each week, you should reach your goals by the end of the year, and, in most cases, exceed them. Focus on goals that you can control in your flash report, such as calls made, doors knocked, mailers sent, or parties attended. The idea is to track only things you have complete control over so that when things do not go your way you do not get discouraged about tracking your numbers. It is also a way to make sure your numbers are improving week over week.

You can do this exercise yourself or contact Diosum Coaching, and we will get you the document you need. If you are doing it yourself, write down on the left side of a piece of paper or, preferably, create a Google Sheet and fill the cells on the left side with items that you want to track, such as: hours worked, hours prospecting, face-to-face contacts, phone calls made, texts sent out, and doors knocked on.

Below are examples of two flash reports:

12/11/23 - 12/17/23	M	T	W	Th	F	Sat	Sun	Totals	Goal	
Doors Knocked	4	3	3	9	40	14	3	76	100	76%
SOI call contacts	3	4	3	14	5	5	3	37	50	74%
Cold call contacts	5	1	6	6	12	0	0	30	25	120%
New Appointments	0	0	1	0	0	0	0	1	2	50%
SOI Text/PM's	4	12	2	15	4	12	2	51	50	102%
Live Video	0	0	0	0	0	0	0	0	1	0%
Hours Prospected	0.5	0.33	2	1	1.2	0	0.5	5.53	5	111%
Total Hours	5	6	6	10	11	3	1	42	40	105%
Contracts	0	0	1	0	0	2	0	3	2	150%

12/4/23 - 12/10/23	M	T	W	Th	F	Sat	Sun	Totals	Goal	
Doors Knocked	0	5	12	9	12	22	0	60	100	60%
SOI call contacts	5	5	5	6	9	7	7	44	50	88%
Cold call contacts	0	0	0	3	3	5	0	11	25	44%
New Appointments	0	0	0	0	0	1	0	1	2	50%
SOI Text/PM's	13	12	2	15	4	12	1	59	50	118%
Live Video	1	0	0	0	0	0		1	1	100%
Hours Prospected	0.5	0.6	2	1	2.1	3	0.5	9.7	5	194%
Total Hours	3	4	8	8.5	9	7	1	40.5	40	101%
Contracts	0	0	0	0	0	1		1	2	50%

Now, to the right of these, you will create a different column for each day of the week, as well as a weekly total column. You will fill these out as you go. At the end of the week, calculate your numbers from each column, and add the results into a weekly total column. Be sure to keep your documents from past weeks, so that you can start to see a pattern of improvement or perhaps catch yourself when there's a declining pattern in those categories that you feel you need to track. Also try to track activities that you struggle to do each day, so this will hold you accountable.

To-do lists. People tend to freeze up and do very little when they're faced with so many things to do that they become overwhelmed. One of the things that holds people back from reaching their numbers goals on any given day is when their mind is too crowded with other items, or when they are so busy trying to take care of their daily to-do list, that time gets away from them, and they no longer have time to make their phone calls or do any of the other things on their flash report. Let's review how to create a master to-do list (or as some people call it, a brain dump), arranged by priority, that will help you overcome this obstacle:

I was taught this process by a mentor who had once read an article about a man who had interviewed fifty self-made millionaires, trying to figure out what made them so productive and successful. The reporter asked each of them what app they used as their to-do list. He was shocked that the large majority of them did not use an app at all (even though many of them were young enough to use apps for almost everything else).

What they actually used was simply a notepad. And most of them said they were most productive when they used a yellow legal notepad, as opposed to a white one. If you do not have time to make it to the store today, go online and immediately order a five- or 10-pack of yellow, legal-sized notepads. If you already have one, great. If not, start with a sheet of paper, and transfer the items over as soon as your yellow notepads arrive.

Let's start with the brain dump aspect of this to-do list. Sit down and give yourself 30 minutes to an entire hour to write down everything you've been wanting to do — all of the monkeys on your back, so to speak. This can be personal or work-related. It can have something to do with relationships. Think about it as trying to empty out your brain with ideas and things you want to accomplish.

An example of this list could be: Teach my son how to ride a bike; buy wife flowers; knock on 100 doors in my neighborhood; do a chest workout; work on listing presentations for 15 minutes; clean out the closet.

This should give you an idea of how we are not just focusing on work. We want everything out and displayed in a list so that all of the things you feel you have to get to will stop fogging up your mind and stop decreasing your productivity. This will often take more than an hour, and you will likely continue adding to it throughout the day. My first time doing it, I ended up with three full pages.

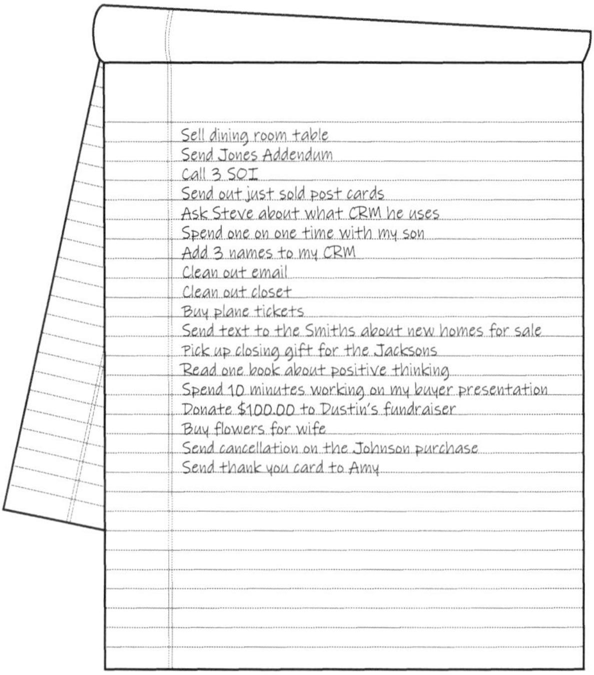

Obviously, you do not always think of things in order of importance. To address that, there is a small, empty column to the left of the left margin. Use that to rate your listed items A, B, C, or D.

A's are things that will either lose you money or get you in trouble if you do not do them. For example, submitting an offer for your client, or responding to a legal deadline.

B's are things that are equally important, but less urgent. They could be sending info on a property to a client who is casually looking. Another example would be teaching your son how to dribble because you haven't been spending enough time with him.

C's are things that are not urgent — cleaning out a closet, for example, but that you'd like to have done soon.

D's are things you need to delegate. These are important. But in order to reach your goals, you need to know how to delegate. Sometimes these are A's, but you still need to delegate them, because they might be something you can hire out and pay someone much less to do than your time is worth.

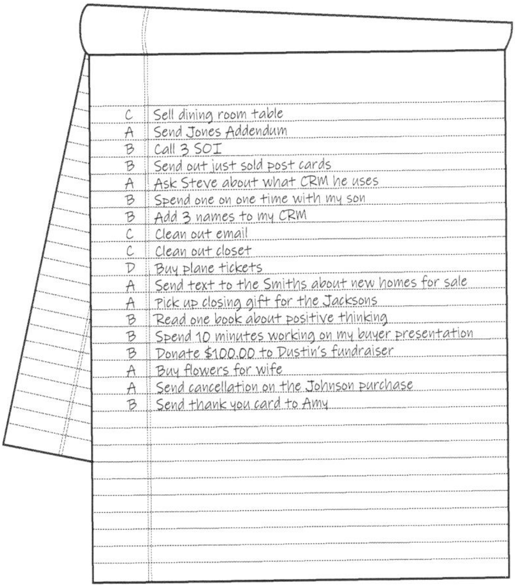

Once you've done that, look over your list and find all the A's. You will now put a number listing next to each of your A's in order of what is most important out of them, for example, 1A, 2A, 3A. You may have to relabel them several times as you go along. Do not hesitate to do this. (This is what I had Taylor do, and why he became so productive.)

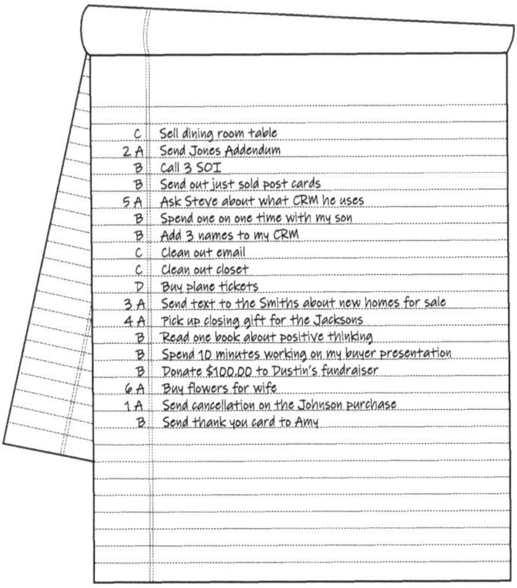

Once you have prioritized your list, insert a deadline for the more important items on your calendar. And if you use a calendar like mine, set some reminders to go off on your phone for those items throughout the day.

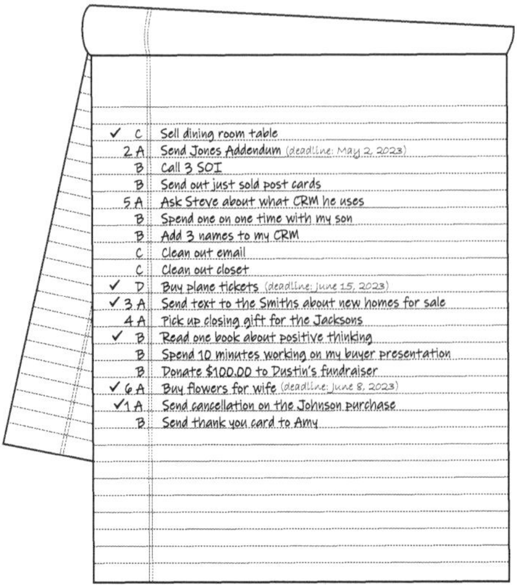

The magic of this list is that whenever you have even just five spare minutes, you immediately know where to put that time, and you will start accomplishing and checking things off the to-do list rapidly. In my case, I ended up getting more done with my to-do list within a week of using this method than I had in the previous year. Make sure as you complete each item that you put a big, aggressive checkmark next to the item. This will release happy endorphins and give you a sense of encouragement to continue.

As you use this method, you will begin to add more things every day. It is important not to make the list messy by extending it to dozens of pages. For this reason, every couple of days rewrite what you haven't accomplished on a fresh sheet and add new items to it. You may throw out the other sheet even if it isn't completed, because you have rewritten the items needed to be done. This also serves as motivation. I got sick of rewriting my C's every week, so I started knocking them out until they were all done.

By doing all of this you will succeed in completing the many tasks that have been fogging up your brain. This will free up time for you to reach the numbers goals you have set for yourself. And, using the tools provided, you will track them accurately throughout each day and each week.

Conclusion

When you put everything down on paper and create a realistic plan on how to achieve every item you've been putting off (and potentially guilting yourself over not doing), you become motivated rather than overwhelmed.

When you prioritize your to-do list and set goals on when to complete each item, you are able to laser-focus on each item until it's completely finished. This clears your mind so you can focus on reaching the numbers goals in your flash report. Your mind will become even more clear, and you will have a deep sense of accomplishment every day as you check off items on your to-do list and reach your numbers goals every day.

Chapter 10

You Have a Sure-fire Sales Process

Let's explore creating a functioning business plan for your real-estate business. This helps you build something that you ***hope*** to succeed at into something you can ***plan to succeed at***. Most REALTORS® do random daily activities and try to implement things randomly to help generate business. <u>A structured plan gives you a method to treat your business as if it were a multimillion dollar company</u>, so it's more likely that you can turn it into one.

The big idea here is that my tested sales process has turned around the careers of many real estate agents and turned former victims into empowered entrepreneurs.

The Business Plan Revelation

I will never forget the first time I created a business plan and established the core principles of my company. I remember because it felt silly making a plan and making core principles when I was literally the only member of my LLC.

The interesting thing is that I did not read it in a book or hear about it at a seminar. I simply thought about it. I think I had been watching TV and saw someone do a sales pitch about their company's business plan, and I thought, 'How in the world can I expect to have a multimillion-dollar business and not at least do some of the basic things that people are expected to do when they start a business?' After outlining my business plan and going through the steps I have put you through, my clarity was tremendous.

For the first time in my career, I did not have to question what was next, or what I should do after I am finished with the present project. That, in combination with my to-do list, really has turned my career around. My productivity has skyrocketed, and the guessing game of daily activities has been eliminated.

When I started using a business plan, I really could see my business as a real business rather than just doing what I could to figure out each day, one day at a time. I would check the plan every morning, and I literally started accomplishing more in a day than I used to in a month by using my structured business plan.

Your Principles and Your Business Plan

Before you create your business plan (which I'll take you through shortly) you should create the core principles by which you will work.

Create core principles. Core principles are three to five words that can be similar to affirmations that you want to base your business practices on. An example would be, "integrity, responsiveness, hard work." Once you've chosen what you think will best set your business up for success, or something you know you need to fix or work on, write down a small description of each of those words. An example would be — Integrity: I will always treat my clients and myself with respect by being honest, forthright, and always prioritizing the truth.

Once you have your core principles, keep them close by. Write them down on a little card to keep in your wallet or use them in your presentations. Most importantly, by refreshing your mind about them frequently, you will start to create a culture in your own mind for what your business is. The first guy I know who did this began with one employee, and now he owns one of the most successful businesses in the world and is the third-largest in that industry.

Create a business plan. Here's how you do it.

Open up a Google Doc, or, if you prefer, a Word document. I always recommend Google, because it's easily accessible and editable on all your devices, including your coach's device, if you share access with him or her. Within this document, create a table with four columns in it.

At the top of the first three columns, pick an area that you want to generate income from.

To do this, reference the list below or check my website or ask your coach to guide you in picking a minimum of three pillars of business, or, in other words, three major methods of generating leads:

- For-sale-by-owner calls
- Cold calls
- Working your SOI (Sphere of Influence)
- Expired calls (when a listing expires
- without selling)
- Door-knocking
- Farming (targeting a specific geographic area)
- Holding events and seminars
- Mailers
- Advertising
- Purchasing leads
- Working with divorce attorneys

Pick the three methods you could see yourself doing daily. Make sure you do your research or talk it over with your coach before you commit to spending time on it. You do not want to start a project and commit valuable time to it, only to switch to a new method when you realize you are not enjoying it.

Say you decide to work your SOI (which I recommend as one of everyone's three pillars). And then you decide also to work Farming and Cold Calls. Put these three items at the top of the first three columns. In the fourth column, write Business Development at the top.
Some people have never used this method. When you hit Tab, it will separate into a new row directly below those categories. In each of these rows, reference your to-do list, or think of new items you need to do in order to succeed in this category.

For example, below "Cold Calls," you could write, "Make 25 cold calls a day, purchase a cold-calling list, block off schedule for cold calling, choose CRM [Customer Relationship Management] software to store leads for cold calling, master follow-up techniques, do online training, or watch YouTube videos on how to improve your cold calling. Role play with a mentor or accountability partner. Practice cold calling." This will be similar to what you did on your master to-do list. You are trying to remember everything you have ever learned and every step you need to take in order to attain success with that lead-generation category.

That's just an example of what one of those columns could look like. It will likely expand down to have a page or more in that single section.

Then press Tab, and for each of the items in that miniature brain dump you just did, put down each step in its own separate box, and break that step down even further into the items you need to accomplish in order to finish that step. Add a deadline at the end of that section, and then move on to the next. An example of this for one of the items above might be, picking a CRM:

- Post on a REALTOR® Facebook page asking for everyone's choice of a favorite CRM

- Read reviews, and pick the top two
- Start pre-trials on the two that sound most appealing
- Complete on or before September 30 (or whatever date you choose)

The goal with this is that you will accomplish everything in these categories necessary for success. Rather than picking up the phone and making twenty-five cold calls and not knowing what to do, you will have set up the infrastructure to take care of those leads and follow up properly — and eventually gain clients and close transactions.

In the Business Development column, do similar things, such as, preparing your listing presentations, reading educational books, attending classes on improving your business, setting up your LLC, hiring an accounting firm, etc.

Here is a sample business plan table:

Cold Calling	**Sphere of Influence**	**Farming**	**Biz Development**
1. Make 25 daily cold calls Purchase cold-calling list 2. Block off schedule for cold calling Choose CRM to store cold-call leads 3. Master follow-up 4. Do online training or watch YouTube videos on how to cold-call better 5. Role play with a mentor or accountability partner 6. Practice cold calling	1. Post two times daily on Facebook and Instagram 2. Write birthday cards 3. Xmas cards in advance 4. Call 5 SOI people daily 5. Throw parties 6. Keep notes in CRM 7. Obtain mailing addresses and email addresses	· Knock on 10 doors daily · Set up twice-monthly mailer · Purchase list of names and addresses in your farm	· Create YouTube page · Create LinkedIn profile · Prepare listing presentations · Read educational books · Attend classes to improve business · Visit with accountant to learn about write offs · Set up a business account at the bank and obtain a business credit card

Make it a goal to check your business plan daily. It is a three step process, and if you just wake up a little bit earlier, if needed, you should be able to check and update your master to-do list, update and look over your flash report, and study your business plan before you begin work each day. This will give you direction and help you stay focused on income-generating activities, as well as on necessary tasks.

With this additional organization, you'll set yourself up with good accountability, and also provide an easy tool for your coach to reference as he helps you build out each category of your business. Doing this will help you approach your business from a strategic and tactical angle, rather than running from one item to another and hoping for success in all of the categories you've been working on.

Conclusion

When people have a detailed business plan and use it as an accountability tool and a way to stay organized and productive, they start to respect their own business more and to actualize the success of their REALTOR® careers.

Chapter 11

Your Mindset Affects Each Step of the Process

Here we're going to explore how you can use goal-setting, creating deadlines, and tracking your progress to keep on top of your changing mindset. You'll read about a woman I worked with who had a victim mentality despite being successful. And you'll get some steps to help kickstart your state of mind into something more positive.

The big idea here is that whether you have a mindset of being a victim, being entitled, or being empowered, it will impact your sales process: Which one do you want to be?

The Ambitious Victim

I worked with Meg, a young woman who said she was ambitious, but had something of a victim mentality. I asked her to visualize the end of the next five years: What does the house look like, What does your car look like, etc. — the same exercise we did in earlier chapters.

Meg's goals were not big: She wanted to have $10,000 in savings and $10,000 in checking, and to have her bathroom remodeled. I had to really dig down with her to get her to understand that there were people in her area making $1 million a year in real estate. I asked, "Are those your goals if you were making $1 million a year? To have $10,000 in savings

and remodel your bathroom?"
Once we got past Meg self-limiting her future goals, it was truly satisfying to see her break out of her shell and admit she wanted big things that she just really didn't think she could have. Meg thought she could never make $100,000 a year in real estate, and even that seemed like a lofty goal at times. Her goals reflected what she thought her maximum potential was in income.

Once we got past her self-limiting beliefs, she admitted she wanted a custom home in a super-nice neighborhood. She wanted to have plenty of money to give to charitable causes. And she wanted to truly pick her schedule and have a team running her business so that she could step away whenever she wanted or needed to.

After helping Meg set up her business plan, create her to-do list, and establish her tracking accountability, she was able to overcome her previous mindset of being a victim. She basically had thought on a daily basis, "I don't know what to do next. My real-estate schooling should have prepared me for how I should actually make money. Nobody's here to guide me. Other REALTORS® are just lucky. I work as hard as they do, but I never have the results they have."

Overcoming these thoughts that had plagued her for many years took time. But through the affirmations and other techniques we have discussed, Meg was able to replace that victim mentality with an empowered and laser-focused mindset.

Today, Meg is doing way better. Because of her higher sales volume, including $1.4 million in sales in one month when Meg closed on three transactions, she was invited to a top-producer lunch. She has also built a new custom home with her husband, very similar, in fact, to the one she had described to me when we were first trying to overcome her self-limiting beliefs.

Affirmations and Your Business Plan

Now that you have a business plan, you should create affirmations that reference it and your master to-do list. (For example, "I am extremely productive," "I cross many things off my to-do list daily," or, "Because of my business plan, I am able to overachieve and earn more money every year," or, "By following all of the steps in my business plan, I now make $250,000 a year.") Remember, all affirmations must be in the present tense.

This would be a good time to revisit the one-, three-, and five-year goals. In reference to your one-, three- and five-year visualizations, spend at least a little bit of time at some point during the morning revisiting your goals that you hoped to reach by the end of this year, and what you want that to look like, and, just as importantly, how you will feel when you reach them.

Then in the evening, take four or five minutes to relax, perhaps in bed as you're falling asleep or as a quick meditation sometime during the evening. Revisit your five-year plan and imagine yourself living in that world. You may also consider daydreaming or going into more elaborate detail on what that five-year life will look like as you drive, rather than thinking of useless things such as sports statistics or political radio talk shows.

Some of these thoughts about your five-year plan could be: 'What type of charities will I donate to at that time," "Who will be in my life and how will I feel about it," "How will my business be growing (maybe I'll become a coach to help some other REALTOR®)." Or maybe you just live in a cabin by the lake in the woods and write novels. Whatever that five-year dream reality is, daydream about all of that instead of things that are unproductive and do not contribute to your success. It is a very effective exercise to replace negative thoughts with dream-building.

You can start each day by remembering and visualizing your end-of-year goals. This helps you be more productive and stick with your business plan, because of how badly you want to reach that goal you have actually visualized, spoken many positive affirmations about, and created a plan to achieve those goals. In addition to this, you should spend moments throughout the day, especially during the evening, establishing in your mind the eventual reality of your five-year dream life. This serves as motivation each day to work toward that one-year goal, leading to the three-year goal, and eventually the five-year goal.

Conclusion

You will never achieve the levels of success or live a life that you dreamed of without visualizing it as possible. In order to accomplish specific things in your career, you must first identify them and create a roadmap to accomplish them by writing down your objectives and concrete plans for your day-by-day activities — or, in other words, create and follow your business plan every day, every week, every month.

Chapter 12

Beginning the Sales Process: Your Long-Range Plans

It is time to take your mindset to a higher level, and to increase your productivity.

You have set up a one-, three-, and five-year plan, which is great. But even those plans should be revisited and revised upward. Don't limit yourself. You also should be doing daily activities that clearly drive you closer to your yearly and long-range goals. Here, we will look at several methods for ensuring you don't get lost in the clouds of your grand vision, but that you do the everyday tasks you need to do in order to make that goal a reachable reality for you.

Before you can get to where you want to go, you need to truly visualize your goal and believe that it is possible. And then you need to adjust your daily productivity levels according to your actual progress, perhaps quarterly, as you move visibly towards that goal. That's how I do it.

Revising Long-Range Goals

I had big long-range goals, but I needed to revise and rethink them several times. The hardest part about this is believing that your five-year plan is possible. Some of my larger thinking was due to my having read the book, The 10 X Rule, by Grant Cardone, whose premise is that you should always take your goal and multiply it by ten.

Before I read that book, I had already set lofty one-year goals for myself. When I found out I should multiply those goals by ten, it was depressing because it was totally unreasonable to expect that I could achieve what I had envisioned by a factor of ten. In order to get a sense, though, of what was possible, I needed to see that others had actually achieved such fantastic goals. I looked for people in my area who had created wealth quickly, just to recognize that this was indeed possible. And I needed to look closer to home: I already knew a couple of people in the area where I lived who had hit it big. One thing these folks had in common was that they had diverse streams of income.

This helped me realize that I needed to consider expanding beyond real estate. I knew I wasn't going to reach my goals by selling $200,000 condos and houses. So I had to come up with a new business plan, one that actually made my long-range goals reachable. This went even beyond the business plan I shared in previous chapters. I had to break each category down to its most basic activities and then expand it out to what I would normally consider a five- or ten-year plan. But in this case, I had to set deadlines for myself that seemed impossible. But at least the plan was in place.

Obviously, the plan would do me little good if I could not begin to truly believe that my huge new goals were attainable. So I had to rethink my affirmations to adjust to the new, more expansive plan I had created. So, again, I turned to the ThinkUp app to write new playlists of affirmations. Slowly, I began to have a small seed of hope that these goals I had planted would blossom into reality.

When I started to really believe it, my mindset on a day-to-day basis completely changed. I stopped wasting my time. I focused more on long-term growth, and I was able to say no to things that did not move me toward my goals. For example, I almost completely stopped working on projects for people who were not committed to using me as a REALTOR®, because I knew that I needed to spend time only on projects that would be contributing to my income and, in reality, I needed at least five or ten hours a week to explore new ideas and opportunities outside of real estate.

I also realized that working forty to fifty hours a week wasn't going to get me to where I needed to be in one year, so I upped my hours to seventy hours a week. This forced me to eliminate time-wasting activities, such as watching sporting events excessively, binge-watching TV shows, and constantly reading articles on my Google newsfeed.

When I realized that my goals were more important to me than these things, I became obsessive to the point that I could not even watch ten minutes of an NBA game, let alone the whole game, without getting antsy and wanting to get back to work. It was really baffling to my group of friends, who sent out texts and started Marco Polo chats about what was going on in the sporting world. I used to have an opinion on every aspect of sporting events, and now had nothing to say and didn't know what they were talking about in general. So, it would come as no surprise that I stopped participating in those chats, as well.

In the end, the biggest change was that I stopped thinking small. When an idea would come to mind that had the potential to really take me to another level, rather than shoot it down as impossible right off the bat, as I used to, I would immediately jump in and develop the idea in my mind and search for a way to make it happen. For example, an opportunity fell in my lap to start a new company from scratch. The upside was very large, but there were a lot of risks and uncertainties, as well. In the past, my fear of failure and my desire to remain comfortable would have stopped the idea in its tracks. But instead I went full steam ahead, and within one month we had the company up and running. Within three months, it was on pace to start generating a profit that will no doubt surpass my real estate income sometime next year. This was only one of the many ventures I had begun to develop once I changed my mindset and expanded my long-range goals.

Expanding Your Goals

If you want to begin expanding your goals and creating a framework for reaching them, you do not necessarily need to do what I did and multiply your goal by ten. Let's at least consider doubling or tripling your current end-of-year goal.

Hopefully, your one-year goal will already lead you to reaching your five-year goal. If you could triple it, it would give you a head start and maybe help you reach your five-year goal in three or four years instead of five.

Begin by writing down your end-of-year income goal at least twenty times a day. Write it in different ways, for example, "I enjoy making $500,000 per year," "I feel so blessed that I make $500,000 per year," "It feels great to make $500,000 a year," and so on. Be sure to do this every day. And when you can, write it down even more than twenty times.

On a separate piece of paper, in neat, readable handwriting, spell out your new end-of-year goals, and how reaching them will make you feel — in the present tense — preferably in a single paragraph. Place the paper somewhere you will see it throughout the day, such as on the wall next to your desk. Or take a picture of it and save it as your phone or computer screensaver.

The power of writing down your goals is that you can begin to taste the reality of it. You probably never write down your daydreams or fantasies, but you should break free of that thinking. Most of us write things down only when they're factual. What you're doing is using the process of writing to chip away at self-limiting beliefs you may still carry about your goals.

Revisit your five-year plan. Cross-reference it with the new one-year goal you have written down. If there is a discrepancy between the two, raise the one that is lower to the one that is higher. For example, if part of your five-year visualization is to live in a $5 million house and to own a $1 million boat, but your one-year goal only has you making $100,000, then you obviously should adjust your one-year goal so it realistically can lead to your five-year goal.

Still, try not to think small. For any self-limiting belief that comes to mind that would potentially derail you from your new mindset or from obtaining your new goals, immediately catch yourself. Replace that thought with the positive version of it, and repeat that to yourself as much as possible.

Take an inventory of your current daily activities. Are they conducive to what you need to do to reach your goals? Or are there things you need to eliminate and replace? Are there small moments when you can squeeze in an extra ten or twenty minutes of work rather than doing a time-wasting activity? Try to commit yourself to living a more constructive life. It's important to look to role models in such moments, to people who have reached the levels of success that you are hoping to reach.

Here's a method to see if you're productive or not. Keep a notepad with you, preferably something small you can carry around in your pocket. Minute-by-minute throughout the day, write down what you are doing, and what you are thinking about while you are doing it.

You should keep quite detailed notes. If you are sitting at your desk looking over your email for work, at 11:05 you'd write down: "11:05, going through emails." Then below that you'd write, "Thinking about the basketball game tonight." If at 11:07 you click on a link and start reading an article, you'd write down: "11:07, reading an article about bitcoin and thinking about bitcoin." Then if you go back, catch yourself, and go back to work, you'd write: "11:11, going through email, thinking about where I'm going for lunch this afternoon."

Keep this log for a minimum of one day, but try to do it for several days in a row. You will likely be surprised how few of your hours are spent being 100% productive and focusing on the task at hand and your larger goal.

By taking corrective steps, you will begin truly to believe in your five-year plan, and your ability to do whatever it takes to achieve it. You will identify and eliminate time-wasting activities and begin to take actions that will move you toward bigger goals. You will stop wasting multiple hours each day on projects or hobbies that will never get you where you want to go.

Conclusion

Two essential elements of reaching greater goals than you had previously thought possible are: one, truly believing in yourself and your capabilities to attain that level of success; and two, doing the daily activities and staying focused and productive.

If you can master these two elements, you will begin to accomplish more in a day than you previously had in a week or a month. This will put you into hyperdrive and propel you toward your goals much more quickly than you had previously thought possible.

Chapter 13

Market Research Is an Essential Tool

Market research gives you not only more to work with as you put together your sales pitches and scripts, it also gives you confidence, and that helps people have confidence in you as a professional REALTOR®. Here I am going to show you why market research makes all the difference in growing your real estate business.

When you know your market, your competition, customers, and potential customers, you can build a more accurate business plan.

My Homemade Sales Process

I created a sales process through my own trial and error.

When I first started trying to venture out and get my own REALTOR® business going, I decided I wanted to do it with for-sale-by-owner properties. I got a list of for-sale-by-owners from my broker and tried calling them. I can't believe now how ridiculous I sounded then.

I'd say, "Hello, are you selling the house on Main Street?"

"Yes."

"Okay, are you interested in hiring a REALTOR®?"
They would say, "No, I am selling by the owner."

"Okay," I'd say, "would you hire me as your REALTOR® if you changed your mind?"

Most would say no, though amazingly a couple would ask, "What have you got? Come and show me."

I had no script, no plan, and no strategy. Because of my persistence, however, I had some success, and a ton of luck. But it was inconsistent. This went on for a couple of years. At the time it wasn't too bad. I figured I had to make several hundred phone calls in order to get a listing, which I did at a huge discount. It was a lot of effort, but it worked, and I made a living.

A few years later, I hired a coach, which changed everything. We created an outline and set up detailed touchpoints for my for-sale-by-owner work. He helped me refine my approach and increased the amount of commission I was asking for.

It was completely night and day.

We started out by researching detailed statistics about for-sale-by-owners in my area. I was shocked to find out that over 85% percent of them ended up hiring a REALTOR®. We also found statistics on how much more their homes would sell for when they used a REALTOR®, as opposed to selling it themselves. After we had this data, we revamped my listing presentation and my script for the phone calls.

After that, I started getting more listing appointments, but I was still listing the properties for a huge discount. I remember the phone call when my coach was going over my income and how many phone calls I was making, and he asked me point blank, "Why aren't you charging more commission?" I said it was the only way to get homeowners to meet with me and sign the paperwork. He challenged me to adjust my script a bit

more by asking for a 6% commission.
Knowing that such a high percentage of for-sale-by-owners would end up hiring a REALTOR® anyway helped me to be a little more laid back on the first call. It was more about gathering information and getting to know them. I would ask questions that would help me approach the second call, such as, "How fast do you need to sell the home? Can you afford to pay a buyer's agent?"

I would also ask more questions to get to know them. One question was: "Why did you decide to sell by owner rather than using a REALTOR®?" Usually, they'd say, "commission." I'd offer them some tips. Sometimes, I would swing by the house and drop off helpful information, such as a packet I had put together of how to sell by the owner. Knowing that they would end up hiring a REALTOR®, I would do multiple follow-ups and get more aggressive on the follow up calls after they were more familiar and more comfortable with me.

Before my conversation with my coach, I would often say, "How about we meet up and I'll give you half price and list your house for 4½ percent," which would give me the meeting right away on the first phone call. However, after I reluctantly agreed with him to try a different approach, I would say, "If you could still net the amount of money you are hoping to, would you have any problem paying me to help out?" Surprisingly, the reaction and the amount of appointments I got was pretty similar; it just took a bit more follow-up. And when I walked into my first appointment expecting to lose the listing because I was now asking for 6%, I was shocked that on the very first try they agreed to pay the full 6% commission.

Doing the research to understand more about the for-sale-by-owner market gave me confidence. Going in with a plan, knowing my numbers, knowing the market, and having belief in what I was saying made all the difference. Having all of these tools and data also helped me create more convincing scripts that strengthened my phone sales.

I now do the same thing whenever I venture into any new lead generating category. Research and positive affirmations are essential first steps. Here's how to go about it.

Getting to Know the Local Market

First, do your local market research. Get on the MLS website and pull the sold reports for the neighborhoods you want to be familiar with, and the active reports. Observe price per square foot per area. MLS has a program that will automatically send you new listings based on the parameters you input. These are called hot sheets.

Create automatic hot sheets to email you these properties daily. This way, you'll begin to feel comfortable with your knowledge about those areas, and you can observe trends and price increases daily. It will also give you a good idea about who your biggest competition is as you start to see the same names pop up over and over again on listings.

Get onto RealtorMag.com and Realtor.com and sign up for their free email lists. If you can afford it, InMan is an excellent website, as well. When they send you emails, be sure to open them and read the articles.

This will help you not only to become knowledgeable, but you will also sound knowledgeable and always have something interesting to say when clients ask you for updates on the market. For example, if your client has two or more REALTOR® buddies, and the client asks each of you what the current market looks like or what the interest rates are, they'll likely get the same general answer from everybody. When you are asked this question, however, you will likely have read an article recently about the subject and can share interesting information that will help you stand out.

For example, I was asked once if it was a seller's market. If they had asked other REALTORS®, they would likely have said, "Yes, it seems to be," or some similar answer. My answer to these potential clients was, "You know, it's an interesting question, because buyers are scrambling to get into a house because of low interest rates, though we are seeing some multiple-offer situations. However, inventory is also pretty high. So I would say perhaps we are in a transition period, where I would not call it a buyer's or seller's market, necessarily. But it is good for both buyers and sellers because interest rates are low and there are plenty of buyers out there looking at homes."

Their reaction to that was actual interest rather than the conversation dying there. We continued talking about it for some time, and their trust in me as a professional clearly increased. They eventually decided to use me as their REALTOR®.

Ask your broker and other real estate agents which books helped them gain the most knowledge the fastest. Make the goal to read at least two books a month. Also, ask the successful agents in your office if they have any other tips for success. (Beware. Everyone has a different approach and will likely tell you theirs is the only one that works; take it with a grain of salt.) Ask for helpful tips for furthering your education plan.

Blunt Feedback

The way I discovered the power of doing research was after my second transaction. My clients were kind enough to leave some very blunt feedback with my team lead. One of the main things they told him was that, although they were glad I never lied about knowing an answer, they were very uncomfortable with my often saying, "Let me look that up" and "I will look that up and let you know what I find." They said, "We would love to recommend him, but he is not very knowledgeable." After I heard this, I did what I described above and started research and reading as much as I could, especially about local real estate.

Only one month later, I met a couple at an open house who were not interested in that house, but who agreed to look at others in the area with me. When we arrived at another house, they asked me a couple of questions about the market, which happened to line up perfectly with an article I had read just that morning on REALTOR® magazine, so I elaborated on the subject as we went through the house. During the showing, they asked me several other questions, and again a lot of answers tied into articles I had read just that morning. I knew statistics and interesting data. I'm sure they were not expecting for me to answer their questions so thoroughly.

As we were leaving the house, they said something that completely floored me, especially considering what had happened with my other client from the previous month. They told me that when they had agreed to see this house with me, they thought that would essentially be the beginning and end of their relationship with me because I was so young. They simply didn't believe I had the experience needed to represent them. After talking with me during those home showings and getting to know me better, they could tell I was an expert and knew what I was doing, and they felt comfortable signing a broker agreement with me.

I was shocked by their reaction, because I was by no means an expert and, in reality, I had only sold a handful of properties. But my research and continuing education on the current market changed my confidence, and this helped clients have more confidence in my REALTOR® abilities.

By continually doing your research, you'll be able to have total confidence in your knowledge and ability to advise and represent clients in your preferred markets. You will not only sound knowledgeable, but you will gain important knowledge about the real estate market so that you can better serve your clients with gusto and contagious confidence.

Conclusion

Once you have a clear understanding of prices and trends in your local market, and a deep well of knowledge about the industry and projections and predictions from experts, you will be better equipped to help your clients. And because of all that, you will have many more clients because they will feel more comfortable and secure working with you as they see your glowing confidence and trust your clearly visible market knowledge. Everybody loves and pays attention to you when they can see you are an expert in real estate.

You may have noticed how I snuck in a positive affirmation just barely. Feel free to add that to your list of daily affirmations ;)

Chapter 14

Generating Leads and Building Your Business

It is important to have a steady flow of leads coming from multiple sources that you feel comfortable working with. Without a proper plan, good scripts, and adequate follow-up, lead generation will easily lead to frustration and uncertainty.

Helping people who have just met you to genuinely trust you will increase the number of clients you have and make transform your lead generation into a much more positive experience.

HOT TIP — One of my main lead-generating sources throughout my career has been open houses. The first REALTOR® I worked an open house with shared how to use a signup sheet, and he gave me the script he used while walking around the home with potential buyers. Now, I continued using his strategy just as he gave it to me for several years, without realizing the percentage of leads and clients I was getting from open houses was extremely low.

Eventually, I attended a seminar on how to generate more business from open houses, and after hearing the speaker's approach and how different it was from what I was trained to do, I did additional research, and my coach and I created a new, improved approach for open houses.

Building Rapport

The biggest change I made was getting rid of the sign-in sheet. So when people walked in the door, I would first shake their hands, ask their names, and introduce myself, without writing anything down, keeping eye contact as much as possible. The goal was to build rapport and trust before I asked for their personal contact and housing needs information.

As we walked through the house, I was friendly and familiar with them, which helped them to feel more at ease with me. We'd talk about why they were moving, how long they'd been looking, and things about their family. I joked around with them and helped them feel I was a friend and a regular guy, not merely a money shark, one of those REALTORS® who cared only about their finances. Once I felt I had accomplished that, I would ask for their personal information so I could send them the property details, and they could get hold of me later, if needed.

As I refined my approach on how to ask for phone numbers and when to ask for it, my percentage of obtaining accurate phone numbers rose to around 95%. Before, I would take down their names, addresses, and phone numbers right away on the sign-in sheet, and, if I had ten visitors, I would get only five or six people to fill it out, and out of those five or six at least two or three would give me a false phone number or not fill in the phone number slot at all. In the end, my new approach made a lot of sense: Why would anyone share their cellphone number or other personal information with somebody they had never met before and with whom they had had no conversation?

One example of this was an open house I was doing on a $1 million home. A couple walked in, and they were extremely cold and reluctant to talk much at the beginning. Clearly, they had been to other open houses and had likely been harassed and chased by shark REALTORS®. As we went through the home, they started to open up a little bit and, seeing how untalkative they were to begin with, I made a special effort to be as relaxed and non-pushy as possible. When we were almost done seeing the home, I reached for my phone and said, "Before I forget, what would be a good number for me to text you my name? That way you can have my contact information. I will also text you a link to the property. This link updates whenever there are price drops and new information. That way you will be able to keep track of what's going on with the house."

I looked down at my phone, and I did not look up until they gave me their phone numbers. Looking up is a form of asking permission. Keeping my head down and starting to type the number implies that I naturally expect the number to be coming, and I am not expecting rejection. They easily shared their number with me, and I ended up becoming their REALTOR®.

Knowing Your Data

Become familiar with and do your due-diligence research on whatever lead source you are planning on using, whether it is open houses, cold calls, or expired listings.

Make sure you know the most recent data, especially any reasonable success percentage that you can expect. This will help you to be less discouraged if you are having what you would have considered poor statistical results. For example, leads from a certain website that many agents in my office purchase, statistically turn into clients only 5% of the time. If I did not know this ahead of time, I would likely have quit, considering that terrible percentage. These types of leads require a lot of follow-up, but are extremely cheap. (I eventually found out that a 5% conversion rate is actually not too bad at all, though).

Develop your talking scripts and read as much material as you can on how to have repeat successes in those lead-generation categories as you possibly can.

In order to develop your own custom talking scripts, look up example scripts online or ask your coach for his favorite talking scripts. But bear in mind that reading directly from those will likely make you sound robotic and disingenuous. So I prefer to use ready-made talking scripts as a guideline or a way of helping train you to respond to future questions. When you make phone calls, keep the script in front of you, but make it a goal not to quote it verbatim or to use it excessively, and you will develop a natural, friendly phone persona that will put your clients at ease.

Take detailed notes, and put all the information you gather from your interaction with leads into your CRM. The more details the better, even things that may not seem important, such as they just got back from their daughter's piano recital, or they mentioned it was their son's birthday yesterday, or they yelled at their dog to shut up. Maybe you learn their dog's name; put that down, as well.

One interesting story about that principle: I was at an appointment with new leads I had never met before. I learned their dog's name was Toby, because they didn't stop yelling at him to be quiet during the entire presentation. As I got to know them better, I found that they considered their dog as their child. They didn't have any kids. Because they had such a love for this dog, I would often start our conversations by asking how Toby was doing, and they would give me detailed answers. They would go on and on about him, delighting in talking about him.

Make sure you have a detailed follow-up plan in place, and, if you're like me, you need to set reminders in your Google calendar to make sure you follow up with your leads. Some CRMs have notifications that integrate with their calendar. And be sure to remember that most leads require seven to ten follow ups before they become committed clients.

As you are gathering information and setting up follow ups, make sure you look for indicators that show whether your leads are worthy of your time or not. You never want to continue following up endlessly with people who have given clear signs they will not be working with you or not be buying or selling a house at all. In other words, know the difference between your hot leads and your cold leads, and make sure you spend the majority of your time on your hot leads.

As you do your research and really get to know your field, you will be comfortable and confident as you start working new and unfamiliar lead sources. With this confidence, you will be able to do what it takes to succeed with many of your leads, or in some cases, abandon certain projects as you realize they do not fit your personality and you won't be able to continue serving them long-term.

Conclusion

With proper research, organized preparation, and diligent follow ups, you will create new opportunities and have success opening up new sources of revenue for your expanding and thriving real estate business.

Chapter 15

Organizing Your Lead Generation

Organizing your leads is very important. Hopefully, I can help you avoid years of trial and error and the mistakes most REALTORS® make that cause them to lose or neglect leads, which in my mind is the same as flushing money down the toilet.

I will also show you how to do this in a way that is absolutely free. I call it the Money List. You'll soon see why this name is spot-on.

The big idea is that when your leads are organized and you are using a system that's easy to understand and work with, the value of those leads will increase exponentially.

Early on in my career, I knew how to get leads, and my team was pretty good at gathering them through open houses and especially through sign calls (based on for-sale signs by our brokerage in front of houses). Because our team leader had many listings, we had a lot of sign ups that generated a lot of phone calls from prospective buyers. The problem was, I would call the lead one time, and if the lead did not quickly seem interested in working with me, I would forget about it and never call again. We did, however, store these leads, but, at that time, we had no system for following up with them after that initial phone call.

Lead Follow-Up

Surprisingly, this is pretty common in the marketplace. Luckily, as part of my ongoing education, I was reading a book about following up on leads. I was shocked to find that most people need to be followed up between seven and ten times before they will even consider buying a property. After reading that, I created what I call the Money List. When I started implementing this list within our team, we started getting more traction with our leads. Our overall sales as a team almost doubled that year, in large part because of the Money List.

Crazily enough, when I left the team, I stopped working the Money List within my own business. I was working a ton of hours and doing everything I thought I needed to succeed. But at one point, my sales were starting to slow down. Because my sales had slowed so dramatically, I was forced to take a hard look at my business processes. Then I realized I had stopped working on the Money List. I dedicated two weeks to pounding hard into my Money List. I added ten or fifteen names to the list from recent leads I had acquired, and I made a goal of reaching each person on the list at least twice during those two weeks.

By the time those two weeks were over, I had over $200,000 in commissions under contract. Granted, this included a couple of huge deals, both of which ended up falling through, but after everything else had closed, I still had the biggest month of my career so far. In fact, I made more money that month than I had made during the entire previous year — that's how important follow ups are. You neglect them at the peril of your financial success.

Your Money List

Here is how to create and manage your own Money List (it's not hard, and it's a gold mine!):

Create a Google Sheet. If you can't do that, use an Excel spreadsheet. (I prefer Google because you can access it on your phone and your mobile Internet, wherever you are.)

Create columns with the following header names: Rank, First, Last, Time, Next, Notes, His, Hers, Price, Commission, Source One, Source Two.

- **Rank:** In this column, you rate each lead on a scale of 0 to 4. I recommend that you use criteria that make sense to you. My criteria are as follows:
    - **Zeros** are current clients, whether they're extremely aggressive, looking to buy a house, or a current listing. I also list brand new leads as Zeros.
    - **Ones** are people who are right on the cusp of being ready to buy or sell, and I am pretty sure they are committed to using me as their REALTOR®.
    - **Twos** are more laid back. They would sell if they could get the right price, which is usually higher than market value. Or they would buy, if the perfect house all of a sudden appeared. But they are in no hurry at all.
    - **Threes** could be considered Ones or Twos. The only difference is that they are not committed to using me as their REALTOR®. They may have openly admitted to working with other REALTORS®, with the logic that whoever brings them the best deal or works the hardest will win their business and help them buy their house.
    - **Fours** I consider to be my pie-in-the-sky, future clients. These are people who may or may not even know that I am a REALTOR®, but I could see them buying or selling in the next couple of years. And I want to start working on the relationship so they can become Ones or Twos as soon as possible.

The key with this ranking system is that when you sit down every day and look at this list, you will contact clients in the order of who will make you money the fastest. With this, you will stop losing leads or neglecting to call them in time. For example, your Zeros are people who you need to work with every day, in order to either close the current deal you're working on with them, receive referrals from them, or, in the case of new leads, transition them into clients. I always have people work their Zeros 100% before moving onto their Ones, and then work on their Ones 100% before moving onto their Twos, etc.

- **First and Last:** Here you write each lead's first and last name. If the lead is a couple, I would put both of their first names in the first name column.
- **Time:** This column is extremely important. What makes this part of the list so effective is that you put here the last date you contacted them. If it's the 19th, as you move through the list calling and texting people, you will put the 19th of the month in each of those boxes. The reason I do this on a Google spreadsheet is because any time you are worried that you are neglecting somebody, you can automatically sort the entire list based on any given column. For instance, if you sort the Time column A to Z, it will automatically move the leads you have neglected the longest to the top of the list. I recommend doing this at least once a week to make sure you are not neglecting anybody for too long.
- **Next:** Fill in with a specific date by which you feel you need to reach out to leads, triggered by your conversations with them. If you are speaking to a Two over the phone, and they say something like, "We will probably start looking a little more aggressively when our son leaves for college in June," then you have a date to put into your list. Additionally, with a lead that strong, I would also put a reminder in the Google calendar to reach out to them.

- **Notes:** I always put the most recent notes first and put the date before each note. So on that phone call regarding the lead who would be more aggressively looking in June, I put the date when I spoke to the client and note that they will start aggressively looking in June when their son leaves for college. Sometimes, when you fill in individual cells in a spreadsheet, such as this Money List, the cells can become dense with text. Make sure to enable the function that shrinks text to fit the space. You may not be able to decipher it at first glance, but when the cell is filled with information, you can easily read it by clicking on the cell, which will open up to allow you to read it in its entirety. Another solution to this problem is to have your CRM up in a different window and take your notes there. Make sure you always pull up your CRM and read previous notes before making phone calls.
- **His and Hers:** This is for phone numbers. I always recommend that you fill out lead phone numbers within the Money List. You never know when your phone may get damaged or lost, or your Google account might get hacked. It's good to have a copy of all the phone numbers of each lead.
- **Price:** Put down the total amount of transactions. For example, if they are just buying and looking in the $300,000 range, I would put $300,000 in that column. But if they were buying and selling, and the house they are selling was listed for $400,000, I would put both prices combined in this column, which here is $700,000.
- **Commission:** I put the estimated commission I anticipate making as soon as I close this client's transactions. This column is meant to be extremely motivating, because if you highlight and drag down a little past all the cells and use the Auto Sum function, it will show you exactly how many commissions you would earn if you were to close on all of these clients. Granted, it is not realistic that you will close all of these clients. But because the list is fluid and you're always

adding people to it or taking them off it, if you work it every day the likelihood of making that kind of money is actually strong.

- **Source One, Source Two:** These sections are important to make sure you're allocating time appropriately. In Source One, I note where the lead came from most recently — meaning, if I had a listing, and they called as a result of a sign they saw, I would indicate "sign call" in this column. For Source Two in that same line, if the listing came because of for-sale-by-owner calls, I would put FSBO (For Sale By Owner) in that column. The benefit of doing this is that you can sort these columns A to Z, just as you did with the Time column, and it will group all of your sections together so that you can see where your leads are coming from. This helps because if you see that 80% of your current leads are coming from SOI (Sphere of Influence) calls, then you can move more of your time over to doing that, and away from things that are not bringing you money or creating new leads.

Below is an example of Money List table:

Rank	First Name	Last Name	Time	Next	Notes	His	Hers	Price	Com-mission	Source One	Sour Twc
2	James	Thorpe	7/10/17	11/11/17	Left VM	801-555-030	801-555-0030	$380,000	$10,000	Geo Leads	past client
3	Jackie	Stiles	8/3/17	12/17/17	Took to See homes	801-555-044	801-555-0044	260,000	7,000	sign call	Past client
3	Brian & Kelly	Ed-wards	11/2/17	12/15/17	Called and talked	801-555-042	801-555-0042	$600,000	$18,000	Open House	Spher
4	Jay	Price	1/15/18	4/11/19	Sent note	801-555-055	801-555-0055	$270,000	$8,000		
4	Michael	Smith	1/15/18	4/10/19	FB PM	801-555-057	801-555-0057	250,000	$7,000	Sign Call	Family
4	Tim	Johnson	1/15/18	4/12/19	Sent text	801-555-059	801-555-0059	500000	$12,000	Sign Call	Sphere
2	Tayla& Jim	Brown	2/2/18	11/6/17	Sent text	801-555-025	801-555-0025	3,000,000	$40,000	Suz	Open House
3	Linda	Monson	2/4/18	12/18/17	Sent text	801-555-045	801-555-0045	$450,000	$13,000	sign call	Sign Ca
3	Angie	Grey	2/10/18	12/16/17	Took to See homes	801-555-043	801-555-0043	$250,000	$7,500	Sign Call	FSBO
0	Jen	Toman	2/12/18	4/7/22	went to take pics	801-555-003	801-555-0003	$240,000	$7,000		

Rank	First Name	Last Name	Time	Next	Notes	His	Hers	Price	Com-mission	Source One	Source Two
3	Walter & Carrie	Tiller	7/12/18	12/24/17	Called and talked	801-555-051	801-555-0051	$250,000	$7,500		
4	Will	Tyson	7/16/18	4/11/19	Called and talked	801-555-058	801-555-0058	$400,000	$12,000	sign call	Sign Call
4	Jannet	Ridly	7/31/18	4/14/19	Left VM	801-555-061	801-555-0061	300,000	$9,000		Sphere
2	Victor	North	8/18	11/8/17	met at open house	801-555-027	801-555-0027	$150,000	$4,300	Referral	Sphere
4	Dylan & Joy	Smith	10/22/18	4/15/19	sent message	801-555-062	801-555-0062	400,000	$13,000		Referral
0	Lucia & Rick	Jackson	12/22/18	2/2/20	Called and talked	801-555-014	801-555-0014	350,000	$10,500	Sphere	SOI
2	John	Winston	01/01/2019	12/17/17	PM on FB	801-555-038	801-555-0038	$1,300,000	$30,000	Open House	SOI
2	Catherine	Jacobson	1/13/19	11/3/17	sent properties	801-555-022	801-555-0022	$600,000	$18,000	Open house payson	SOI
1	Tina	Gibson	1/30/19	2/6/20	Called and talked	801-555-018	801-555-0018	$180,000	$5,000	SOI	
3	Robert & Nicole	Ivins	2/2/19	12/20/17	sent properties	801-555-047	801-555-0047	$300,000	$9,000	Cold Call	Open House
0	Dennis & Kathy	Oliver	2/11/19	2/20/19	sent text	801-555-013	801-555-0013	$340,000	$5,000	Sign Call	Open House
2	Dan	Ivy	2/11/19	11/12/17	met at work	801-555-031	801-555-0031	$250,000	$8,500	Referral	Referral
2	Christiana	Kline	2/18/19	11/5/17	referred by Jack	801-555-024	801-555-0024	$300,000	$9,000	Referral	Sign Call
1	Debbie	Vaca	2/22/19	2/5/20	sent message	801-555-017	801-555-0017	1,300,000	$30,000	FSBO	Facebook
2	Mike	Jacks	2/22/19	12/13/17	Called and talked	801-555-034	801-555-0034	$200,000	$6,000	Facebook	Refferal
2	Clint	Arm-strong	2/22/19	12/15/17	Called and talked	801-555-036	801-555-0036	1,000,000	$30,000	FSBO	Referral
2	James	Fillmore	2/22/19	12/11/17	met at dinner	801-555-032	801-555-0032	$350,000	$10,000	Networking	SOI
2	Natalie	Waters	2/22/19	12/18/17	sent properties	801-555-039	801-555-0039	500,000	$15,000	Sphere	
3	Jyle & Jason	LeBaron	2/22/19	12/23/17	Took to See homes	801-555-050	801-555-0050	$450,000	$11,000	Sphere	Referral
2	Shirly	Rawley	3/22/19	12/14/17	met at party	801-555-035	801-555-0035	$400,000	$12,000	Friend	cold call
2	Eva	Miller	3/22/19	11/10/17	UC need to call	801-555-029	801-555-0029	460,000	$5,000	past client	FSBO
								$15,980,000	$389,300		

I highly recommend you start each day by working this list, until you feel that it is complete and you are on top of each lead. If this means you need to get to the office 30 minutes earlier, or wake up an hour earlier, it is worth doing. Over time your Money list will grow. At one point in my career I had over 80 people on it.

By doing all this, you will stop losing leads after putting in all the work to obtain them. And you will follow up an adequate number of times and start converting leads into buying clients at a much higher percentage. That's a good reason for calling it the Money List, right?

Conclusion

REALTORS® who track their leads, organize them, and follow up relentlessly will quickly discover that they always have plenty of opportunity to make a lot of money in real estate. And if you do this consistently, you will see how surprisingly simple it is to reach your goals.

Chapter 16

Qualifying Leads

Many times when REALTORS® obtain a lead, they are confused about how and when to follow up, how to categorize leads, and how much time to spend on any given lead.

I will now show you how you can qualify leads and maximize your time with them in order to ensure that as many leads as possible turn into sales, referral sources, and, in some cases, actual friends.

I will also discuss the importance of using CRM (Customer Relationship Management) software, which is software that's essential to your continuing success in developing leads and cultivating clients.

I have found that success in this business is longer lasting and more enjoyable when your clients become great friends. How awesome is it that you can literally spend your day talking to and working with your favorite people, and make a great living doing it?

If this is your goal, you need to remember that each lead and each potential client represents someone who could become a friend. When you treat your leads this way in a genuine manner,you will build trust more quickly, and you will have a high conversion percentage.

When you follow up and spend your time cultivating your best leads, and stop wasting your time chasing leads that will likely result in frustration, you can build a pipeline for your business around people you enjoy working with. And those people will refer you and continue to use you as their agent for the rest of their lives. This will help you enjoy the business more and take away the frustration and anger that comes with spending a lot of time on wishy-washy leads.

Maximizing Leads

The day I stopped chasing every lead was when I really started to maximize my lead potential. I remember meeting someone who told me he was working with three other REALTORS®. He said whoever found him the best deal would earn his money.

Normally, I would jump at the chance and go straight to work, potentially wasting hours and hours, only to have one of the other agents get lucky and find the ideal home before me. Instead, I told this potential client that if he hired me I would work my tail off, and I truly believed I would be able to find him any home anybody else could, and more.

I told him I would love to work with him and represent him exclusively and did my best elevator pitch on why this was in his best interest, rather than working with all four of us simultaneously. He tried to pressure and bully me into playing along with his game. In the end, I ended up shaking his hand and wishing him the best of luck, but telling him I could only work with him if he was willing to commit to me.

Over the course of the next week or so, as I put my time toward cultivating my other leads and working on other projects, I was amazed to think of all the time I would have been spending trying to outrun those other REALTORS® to try to win that sale. I ended up getting several solid leads that week when I would have been wasting my time with him. More importantly, it felt so good to respect myself and know my value. When I turned down his business, it built my confidence, and helped me value my true worth and the value of my professional time.

Qualifying Your Leads

Here are several strategies you can use to qualify your leads in order to make sure they are worth your time.

- First, the questions you should ask: Next time you speak to a lead, try asking several of these questions to get a good idea whether this is the type of lead you want to pursue:
    - How long have you been looking?
    - Have you worked with any other REALTORS®?
    - Do you have a house to sell as well?
    - How many homes have you bought and sold in the past?
    - Have you already spoken to a lender and gotten prequalified?
    - Why are you moving?
    - How many houses have you seen?
    - How soon do you need to make your move?

  The answers to these questions can help you understand how serious they are in general, but also whether they are already working with other REALTORS®. If, for example, you ask how long they have been looking, and they say two years, you're in for a long process that will result in a lot of frustration. This is especially true when you ask them if they have worked with other REALTORS®, and they say that several have been sending them properties to consider.

  This usually means that they are willing to throw you in the mix and that they do not value any of the REALTORS'® time. If they have a house to sell and you find they want a lot more than it is worth to make the next transaction work, there is another obstacle that may be frustrating to get over. I am sure you can come up with more questions to help you determine the quality of your leads.

We've gone over how to work your Money List, but what do you do with long-term storage? What will you do with people who don't want to buy or sell anytime soon, but who could be clients you'd like to keep in touch with and cultivate? This is where your CRM comes in.

- To get started on your CRM, take all of your current contacts and create a Google spreadsheet with key data such as first name, last name, email address, phone number, address, city, state, zip code. This is sufficient to get started. The good news is that if you have a Google account and your contacts are uploaded into it, you can actually go through that directly from Google on your phone any time, anywhere, and label which contacts you want included in the list and generate a spreadsheet.

  This is where you want to spend some time choosing a CRM for long-term client data storage. I recommend speaking with your coach and identifying the top two CRMs he recommends for you and signing up for a free trial on both of them.

  During the two- to four-week free trial period, make sure you try out as much of the functions within the CRM as possible. Upload your client database into it, and see which system is easier for you to use and more efficient for your personality type. If neither of the systems works for you as much as you would like, try another one until you find the right one for you. It is important that you pick one quickly, preferably within one week.

- Key things to look for in a CRM:

  - Make sure they are not overdoing it with functions. You

don't want a CRM that attempts to do everything, because that may make it too busy and not very user friendly.

- Look for a CRM that has reminders that can link with your Google calendar.
- Keep track of data such as pets' names, children's names, birthdays, and hobbies.
- Is the data entry aspect easy?
- Is the CRM's mobile platform user-friendly? (You will most often enter leads on your mobile device, so be sure to test it diligently from your mobile device.)
- Check the reviews and make sure that other REALTORS® like the CRM and specifically give it good marks on user friendliness and simplicity.
- Make sure it can easily create new labels or tags for clients in the database.
- Does it integrate with lead-generating companies such as Realtor.com or Zillow?

- Once you have chosen a CRM, then put all of your new contacts into it and create labels for everybody in the database. The rating system will be different than on your Money List. That's because this rating system has nothing to do with the likelihood of buying or selling in the next several months, but with the quality of the contact in the long run. Label client entries as follows:

    - **A's.** These are clients you are almost 100% certain will buy or sell with you for the rest of their lives, or who you want to become part of this category. They are also your biggest referral partners and cheerleaders. For example, anyone you've helped buy or sell already would qualify as an A; also, anyone who has ever referred you to someone else. You will also want to put in this category people you consider great friends you think would also become great clients. Your goal with the A's list is to be in front of them at least four times a month in the form of in-person encounters, mailers, Facebook interactions, or phone calls. These are the people you invite to all of your client events, and on whom you focus the majority of your calls, texts, and small party gatherings.

- **B's.** These people are similar to A's, but you are unsure whether you can get them to that point or, whether the relationship could ever be strong enough to be considered an A. You may still get referrals from these, and many B's will end up buying from you, at which point you will convert them to A's. You want to make sure you are in front of the B's at least once a month, but twice a month is optimal. You may not invite your entire B list to all of your client events, but you will invite your entire B list to larger events that generate less money per person.

- **C's.** These are made up of any lead or contact that you would be okay working with. You will not contact C's often. C's might be contacts you send one mailer to quarterly from an email list. More often than not, C's do not result in a lot of business, but the bigger you build your database and you have several hundred or even several thousand in your C's category, you will eventually see business trickle in from C's as long as you consistently keep up with them.

You may be wondering how to gather data such as email addresses, phone numbers, and physical addresses. We will show you how to do that in the coming chapters.

It is important to note that if you are unable to choose a CRM, or even if you are in the process of finding a CRM, you can use Google as an adequate CRM for almost all of your basic needs. Within Google you can save birthdays, save notes, put down spouse names, and even assign labels. I would recommend you go through your Google contacts at the beginning of this process and find everybody you would want saved as an A and label them in Google. If you are like me, you will go through all of the contacts. Within my Google listing of clients , I have every single contact separated into its appropriate category.

As you meet people and encounter new leads, you will know how to identify their short-term and long-term value, and to categorize and follow up with them in a way that will help you stop wasting time on low-quality leads and non-loyal buyers or sellers. And so you will spend your time building stronger, longer-lasting relationships with people who will refer you to others and use you for years to come.

Conclusion

When you ask the appropriate questions and truly learn how to qualify and categorize leads, your job will become much more enjoyable, as you choose the people you want to work with rather than chasing every lead and opportunity regardless of whether you feel respected or are building a long-lasting relationship or not. And you will also make more money, because you'll spend more time and effort on people who will refer you to others and use you again and again in their real estate interests.

Chapter 17

Approaching Contacts in Your Database

Intention makes a huge difference when approaching your leads. Will they become just a client? Or a friend? Or both? As I mentioned earlier, I prefer that they be both friends and clients.

Your mindset in regard to your contacts and leads will show in the way you approach them. If your mindset is right, each time you contact or interact with your leads, the relationship will grow, and their loyalty will become stronger. If your mindset is wrong (that is, merely greedy), then people will gravitate away from you, and you will experience heavy turnover and few referrals within your business.

The big idea is that approaching your leads in the right way is the difference between cultivating them or alienating them. Looking at your leads as friends, as well as people you want to have a lifetime relationship with, will make you treat them differently than if you look at them solely as a source of income.

Beyond Transactional Thinking

A few years into my career, I was sick of working my business on a transaction-to-transaction basis. That is, I felt I was starting to look at friends and new contacts only as a way to generate money, and it was preventing me from creating genuine connections and long-lasting friendships. I also

found it was hurting my current relationships.
For example, I had one specific friend, Tyler, whom I continually tried to talk to about buying a house. I knew he was in a position to do that, and it would be good for him financially, but in reality I was thinking more about myself and my home and my upcoming mortgage payments and what his buying a house could do for me.

The situation was creating frustration for both of us. This, in combination with the fact that I was not making a lot of money, had me rethink the direction of my career.

I decided to spend a couple of weeks soul-searching and trying to figure out what I really wanted to do with my life and my time. I asked myself, if money wasn't an object, what would I do with my time and how would I want to spend the rest of my life? I found that the answer was that I would want to get to know more people, build stronger connections with my current friends, truly become a genuine friend, and expand my Sphere of Influence (please also review my discussions on the big What-Why, in Chapter 6, and on mindset, in Chapter 7).

Luckily, I was able to put two-and-two together and realize that this was actually the best way to grow my real estate business. All I had to do was change my mindset.

From that point on, I made it a goal to always keep my clients' best interests at heart and focus on building the relationship, rather than just on greedily generating sales through my Sphere of Influence (SOI). I firmly chose to live my life as best as I could by believing that people and relationships were more important than money. There is a big difference between saying this and truly living it, and people can tell. When I started to truly live this principle within my real estate business, I found that clients were more loyal to me, and I started to get referrals and began not only to strengthen my current relationships, but to acquire new friends, since many of my clients became some of my best friends. This trend has continued through to today, and if you had me create a list of my top 25 friends at this moment, I wouldn't doubt that 15 or 20 of them had been clients before they became friends, or they became clients and friends at the same time.

Building Relationships

Here are a couple of simple exercises. Hopefully, they will help you get a better idea of where your mind is and start putting you on a path to building relationships within your business:

- Take ten names from your A list and write them down on a piece of paper.

- Next to each name, write three things you love about that person, and also write down what you want the relationship to look like in ten years. If you cannot complete this with each one of these people, either take them off the list and move them to your B list or make a commitment to think about it and have better answers tomorrow.

- Goal: If you decide you don't care to have a relationship with those ten people in ten years, or you can't think of anything you like about them, it shouldn't be a relationship you cultivate. If you don't want a relationship with them, they shouldn't be on your A list. In reality, unless these people are constantly referring others to you, they should be on your B or C list.

- Next, write five sincere texts or handwritten notes to each person on the list expressing gratitude for their friendship. An example might look like, "David, I just wanted to reach out to you and thank you for what a great example you are in my life. I have always appreciated your pleasant personality, and how hard you work for your family. I'm grateful to have a friend like you."

- In your CRM, find a place within each contact's data screen to put down their preferred method of contact. It can frustrate people and hurt relationships if you continue to contact them in a way they don't prefer. For example, many people who have been using cellphones for a smaller percentage of their life prefer a phone call over a text message, whereas a surprising number of millennials and Generation Z'ers would much prefer a text, and some would even consider it odd to receive a phone call from you. Make sure you contact people in a way they are comfortable with and prefer, as you follow up over the course of your relationship with them.

- As you follow up in interactions with these people, focus your conversations on them, their family, their work, and their hobbies. As you do this, you will get to know them better, and you will be talking about their favorite subject, themselves. This will help you have plenty of data and notes to add to your CRM, and it will also help them feel a stronger connection with you, because most people that they speak to besides you will want to talk about themselves and will not make your friends feel very important. By contrast, they will feel that you are extremely interested in their lives, and because you take great notes you will remember things about them that others forget.

- I cannot tell you how many times I have called a past client or someone with whom I have a real-estate-based relationship, and they will immediately jump into explaining where they are at with their current real estate needs. For example, a past client-friend will start the conversation after I ask how they're doing, with, "We're doing pretty good, still enjoying the house," not wanting to make a move anytime soon. Or someone who I have recently met and is now a lead will say, "We're doing well, but not ready to pull the trigger yet." After they say something like this, I will usually say, "Oh, that's not why I called, I just wanted to check in and see how your family is doing." Sometimes I will say something to get a laugh out of them, such as, "Hopefully, you do not feel insulted by this, but I was bored and just wanted to talk to a friend." Sometimes these conversations launch into very valuable relationship-building opportunities, and it helps them realize that I am actually their friend, not just because I want to help them with a real estate transaction.

As you do this, you will start to build genuine friendships with your top clients and contacts. These friendships will result in higher loyalty and more referrals. You will also begin to fill your database with helpful information and contact people in a way that is most comfortable for them.

Conclusion

When you approach leads and current contacts with the correct mindset and in a method that they prefer and feel comfortable with, you are building the foundation for success in the relationship. They will begin to like you and trust you more and more, as they feel that you are interested in them, and that you truly care about the relationship as more than just a means to a financial end. This will result in lifelong relationships that generate a lot of business for you as by products of your patiently cultivated friendships.

Chapter 18

Master Your Follow-Ups

Follow-up is the key to success when you are working, not only with leads, but people in your Sphere of Influence. It is essential that you stay top of mind with everybody in your database, because they will easily forget all about you in the spur of the moment when they decide to make a move, if they have not seen your face or spoken to you within the last couple of weeks.

While it's important to approach leads in the right way, following up is where you make the biggest difference in cultivating a potential client. I would say without hesitation that someone who has very bad sales skills and is terrible on the phone will have a more successful career than someone who is a whiz kid on the phone if the person with the terrible sales skills is a master of follow-up and the whiz kid is not.

Continuous Follow-up

I have many stories about how continuous follow-up has paid huge dividends in my career.

Here are two of those stories:

Recently a couple who had texted me over five years ago because of one of my sign riders (my name and phone number on a lawn sign) just barely closed on a house this month. I had been following up with them for all of that time. I texted, Facebook messaged, or popped by their house every month during that entire period. After collecting my meager commission on the very affordable house they bought, I looked at the time I had spent and questioned if it was worth all of that effort. Then I realized for three reasons that it absolutely was.

First, I consider those two to be great friends now. I honestly look forward to a lifetime relationship with them.

Second, even factoring in all of that follow-up, I still made more per hour than most college graduates would make, because, in reality, follow-up usually doesn't take much time at all when it's a text message or a quick phone call.

And third, they have already given me two names of friends who are looking to buy or sell. So they have become amazing referral partners.

The crazy thing is, even after all of the follow-up throughout the years, the month before they started looking for a home I called them to see how they were doing, and they were literally about to sign up for a special program through their employment to buy a house, which would have prevented them from working with me. This had nothing to do with me or them not being satisfied with me as their potential REALTOR®. It's just that, believe it or not, after almost 100 follow-ups, in that moment when they saw the program with the perks, they forgot I was even an option. Thank goodness I called them that week! They immediately chose to work with me, without any convincing needed. This experience reestablished in my mind why it is so essential that we follow up weekly with clients. If I had called them three weeks later, rather than when I did, they would already have signed up for the other program.

The other story is about one of the REALTOR® agents I've been training recently.

He was having a similar experience with a lead he obtained about four years ago. At that time he was just starting out, so I had him do an open house on one of my listings.

I gave him instructions on how to collect leads and do proper follow-up. Several years went by, and I had forgotten that he had ever even done an open house on one of my listings. A couple of months ago, he called me out of the blue and told me that the same couple had just bought a house through him.

I congratulated him on his fantastic follow-up and asked him what he did. He told me that for that entire four years, he sent them properties at least once a month, put them on his mailing list, invited them to client events, and called them on each of their birthdays. His commission will be over $15,000, and, more importantly, when I asked him if it was frustrating waiting that long, he said, "Not at all. Because they are now among some of my closest friends."

How to Create a Framework for Follow-Up

Now that you have a better understanding of how to cultivate leads, we will revisit one of the lists you created earlier. The things you have just learned will help create a framework for your follow-ups.

Open up your Money List. In the column labeled Time, hit the dropdown arrow and sort the column A to Z, so that the leads you have not contacted in a while are moved to the top.

Start there and do the most aggressive follow up you feel comfortable with. For some leads, this might mean a phone call or even a pop-by at their house. For others, you may not be that far along in the relationship or process and a text or email might be more appropriate.

As you contact clients, update that column with the day's date. Make sure if you're doing phone calls that you leave a voice message so they know that you got in touch with them that day. Same with a pop-by. Do not make time to drive to someone's house if you do not take anything with you to leave behind. Don't overthink it. I've seen agents take candy bars with their business cards taped to them.

Your list will likely have fewer than a hundred people on it and most likely will have only thirty or forty. So work hard to review this list every day. Optimally, you will be in front of each person on this list every week, in one form or another. Remember that your 3s and 4s on this list, and even some of your 2s, are people you don't even want to contact every week. In those cases, you want them on a list for targeted Facebook marketing, so they at least scroll past your ad several times a month.

Still having trouble knowing what to say in these follow-ups? Get with your coach or mentor and go over a detailed follow-up strategy. If you do not yet have a coach, do your best to find one for advice on YouTube and Google Search. Just make sure you include "Real Estate Agent" in your search. Spend some time researching these strategies and put together your own follow-up game plan.

You will be laying the groundwork for relationship building that will allow your leads to think of you as a friend. You will never allow so much time to pass between contacting your leads that they use a different REALTOR® simply out of convenience, when they would rather have used you if they had only remembered.

Conclusion

Agents with the best follow-up strategies, who stick to them, will win the lead game more often than those who don't use them 100% of the time. If you can become a master of follow-ups, it can make up for many other deficiencies you may have, such as sales skills, comfortability on the phone, and even not being much of a people person.

Chapter 19

Following Up with Leads and Prospects

You can transition your leads from listings into clients at the same time as you take great care of your sellers. We will teach you how to follow up with leads in a manner that will make them feel comfortable and relaxed as they get to know you better.

Following up the right way makes you memorable. It also makes it easier to build a solid relationship with your clients. When you learn people's preferred methods to be followed up with, as well as their speech patterns and personality, your follow-up with specific leads become more and more tailored to them. This makes them feel more comfortable with you every day.

Efficient Follow-Up

When I first started becoming efficient in follow-ups, it was because of a seller who insisted we keep track of and share with him our every lead and that we provide notes and proof of follow-up using a Google spreadsheet.

At the time, we were a bit put off. We felt that was a waste of time to follow up with every single lead, given that many leads do not qualify or are just looky-loos (contacts who like to look at homes, but have no intention of buying). But we complied with our seller's demand and gathered all of the information. At the very first open house I did on a certain property, a man called Dane came through. He zipped through the house in less than a minute, made several rude comments about the poor craftsmanship of the house, and how overpriced the house was, and then he started out the door. I quickly asked for his personal information and, surprisingly, he gave it to me. Per the seller's request, I called or texted him once a week for the next several months while that property was listed.

Lo and behold, three months later, during one of my follow-up calls, he said he'd like to see the property again. I scheduled a private tour. This time he was much nicer and stayed for about 30 minutes. He had decided on an offer amount and, by the end of the meeting, he told me he could close quickly. We were under contract that evening.

You are probably wondering how this happened. As it turns out, our listing was the first home Dane had been through. The last time he had bought a property had been nearly 10 years earlier, and he had no idea what the current market asked for as far as price or conditions in that area.

During the three months that I was following up with him, he was regularly attending other open houses and slowly started to see that our listed home was actually pretty reasonably priced, and its condition was similar to other homes in the surrounding area. That, in combination with the fact that it was in walking distance of his job, and the fact that there was a pesky REALTOR® (me) who would not stop calling him every week, led him back to the house and resulted in a sale. Needless to say, my business partner and I had to eat a lot of humble pie and start implementing that same degree of follow up with every listing we had from that point on.

It should be noted that as I followed up with Dane, I specifically asked him his preferred method of contact. He said he was okay with a phone call here and there, but that he preferred text. Because I contacted him in a way that he preferred, he was willing to endure my follow-up longer than he likely would have if I had been constantly calling him.

Following the Leads

So where do we keep track of the leads that you get from your listings? I prefer to do so within my Google spreadsheet that we used earlier, called the Money List.

Now let's create a new tab in your Money List. At the top of the new page, make sure the order is exactly the same as the order of your CRM, so that you can easily copy and paste over the leads.

Then name the new tab after one of your listings, if you have one, right now.

You should create a new tab for each of your listings Whenever you get a phone call or a text, or when you meet someone at an open house, input their information as a new lead inside the tab for that specific property.

Now that you have all the leads for each specific property in a spreadsheet, it will enable you to follow up weekly with them as a benefit to your seller, and also as a benefit to yourself, as some of these leads may end up using you as their REALTOR®.

NOTE: Be sure also to enter the names and numbers of other REALTORS® who call on the property. Your responsibility as a good listing agent is to follow up with them, as well. Create some sort of indicator that specifies which client has a REALTOR®, who is already represented, and who is not represented. In my Money List, I have a column labeled Agency; when the lead has an agent, I put them in that section, or, if they're unrepresented, I put them as 'unrepresented.'

As you follow up on your listings and leads in general, whether they be on your Money List or simply contacts in your database, be sure to find a way to casually ask them how they prefer being contacted.

With leads, you need to be a little more careful with the

question, and sometimes you need to feel it out without asking it, so you don't give them the opportunity to say, "Don't contact me." With people you are working with and friends in your database, it's easier to say, "I want to stay in touch. Do you prefer phone calls or email?" They will appreciate your honesty and will be okay with your frequent contacts.

In your CRM or in a column of your Money List, be sure to add a label that allows you to specify their preferred method of contact, since you will undoubtedly forget over time as you accumulate more and more leads.

With a combination of frequent follow-up and following up in a way that people are comfortable with, prospects will feel less frustrated with the frequency of follow-up and also be more comfortable with agents reaching out to them regularly.

Conclusion

Real estate agents who pay close attention to the preferences of their leads and clients will always come across as helpful and friendly, rather than annoying and pushy. Also, agents who follow up incessantly with leads on their listings will not only generate more business for themselves, but their listings will sell faster, which will please their sellers and make for better experiences during the listing period.

Chapter 20

Creating Follow-Up Through Lead Generation

When you call your leads and your Sphere of Influence, it is essential they feel that you are not wasting their time. If you can make leads feel you are a great resource, and that you are actually helpful and always providing them value, the bond will grow stronger, and this will result in more sales and referrals.

When you create opportunity, you will be able to pleasantly surprise your leads through your proactive approach to solving their problems or addressing their issues.

A great example of this happened one time when I was making calls to my past clients. I was speaking to a woman I had helped to buy a house about two years earlier. She and her husband are among my clients who also happened to have become close friends with me. Our phone call that day was very casual. I was just checking in on the family to see how they were doing.

As we spoke, the conversation veered toward retirement and her and her husband's retirement goals as a family. This happens to be a good strategy in a conversation — when you are talking about certain personal developments in people's lives, your interest in them will often lead to opportunities for more business. You likely have an advantage here, because you know a lot more about your clients and friends than many of their close friends know.

Retirement Planning

She expressed frustration that even though they had been married for nearly thirty years, they did not have an impressive retirement plan. She mentioned that for a long time she and her husband had been wishing they could invest in real estate, but could never save up enough money. You see, his job barely provided for their needs and a little extra to put away in the retirement fund, which often got dipped into for emergencies.

Since I had sold them their house, I knew it had gone up in value by nearly $80,000.

I explained to her that she could pull the equity out of her home, and, if we found the right property, she could have enough cash flow to cover the home equity line of credit payment, as well as to provide themselves with a bit more cash flow. Most important, they could have a rental property that was being paid off by renters, while setting themselves up for a retirement plan.

They quickly asked me for contact information for good banks to get a loan. We quickly found several great options for a rental property.

Fast forward several months later.

They now feel much more comfortable with their financial future. And they are incredibly grateful and extremely complimentary of my creative solution to a problem they had been struggling with and had frustrated them for the last 10 to 15 years. They are well on their way to obtaining a second property within the next couple of years, and we have them on an accelerated plan to pay off the properties. They will likely retire with several completely paid-off properties that will provide very good cash flow.

Creating Opportunities

So how do you create opportunities such as the one I just spoke about? Here are the steps for doing just that:

- Go to your Money List and your CRM database; pull up the list of people you are going to be following up with today and the people you are going to be calling.

- Write each of their names down on a piece of paper and spend at least one minute brainstorming about each specific client and what their potential needs could be before making the call. Brainstorm also about creative solutions for those needs.

    - This does not mean that you need to bring up those ideas in your call. Rather, it will set you up for success if the call slides into that area. Hopefully, if you have a list of 10 people you were planning on calling that day, at least five or six of those needs may be real-estate related, and it may nudge them toward doing a transaction.

- Do not limit problem-solving to real estate. Your goal is to be a long-term resource in their life. If one of their needs is choosing where they want their kids to go to high school, you could easily provide them resources about local high schools and direct them to school websites. Whatever the case may be, your goal is that when they get off the phone with you they feel you are a good friend and that you always seem to be able to help them with whatever their current needs are, regardless of whether it's real-estate related or not.

- This quick brainstorming session is great practice to continue doing throughout your career. There is nothing wrong --- and everything right --- with spending some prep time reminding yourself and thinking about each person before you call them.

- A good aid in doing this is taking good notes during phone calls. So make sure you take the time to take good notes during or after each of your calls.

Your follow-up phone calls and your random phone calls to your Spheres of Influence will become far more productive, meaning your clients will feel that you are constantly helpful and truly care about their needs.

Conclusion

Real estate agents who became a trusted resource and who build a reputation for themselves as somebody who truly cares about the needs of their clients, whether they are real-estate related or not, not only create a solid relationship with their clients, but are in a position to be the go-to person when any needs or problems arise.

If your clients think about calling you for advice on restaurants, tax attorneys, or even pestcontrol companies, then they're that much more likely to call you when they're about to do something in your specialty field of real estate.

Chapter 21

Continuing Client Relations

Here we will teach you how to become a good friend to an expanded list of people, which may seem unrealistic at first glance. All of us have five or ten close friends whose personal details we're familiar with. How many more referrals, and how much more business would you get, if you could expand that list to 100 people or more?

You're building a two-sided relationship that's both friendship and business, where everyone benefits. You can change people's attitudes from considering you just as a salesman into knowing you are also a friend whom they can trust.

As you build a true relationship with your clients, you will run into several roadblocks. The biggest and hardest to overcome is remembering details of their lives. In order to not only appear as a true friend but to become a true friend, you need to be invested in people's lives and remember the important details about them. At first, it will seem impersonal, but the best way to do this is through your CRM.

I remember the first time I started adding advanced information into my CRM. It felt a bit cold. I looked up details about people's lives on Facebook, added the details to my CRM, and then tried to reference them via text messaging or on a phone call. The more I did it, though, the more I realized that because I do not have the ability to spend hours and hours with each of these people, this was the only way to truly get to know them. At this point, it became fun. I felt like a detective fishing through people's Facebook profiles and getting to know them better.

Growing Friendships

As my database began to hold more personal information about people, such as hobbies, names of children, where they worked, etc., it made my friendship with each client grow at a much more rapid pace. I felt closer to them because I was more involved in their life, even though at this point it was primarily a one-sided relationship.

After I started doing this, I ran into one of my contacts whom I had not seen in almost two years. I did not have her phone number saved, and we were not yet friends on Facebook. But as a habit, I reviewed everybody in my CRM regularly, regardless of whether I spoke to them recently or not.

When I saw her, we exchanged pleasantries, and then I asked, "Have you had any good seafood or been to any masquerade balls recently?"

She was taken aback that I had remembered those details about her life. Several years earlier, I had stumbled into her while I was taking care of business in a building where she had an office. She was eating seafood at her desk, and I saw a masquerade mask on her bookshelf behind her desk. The fact that I remembered these details impressed her so much that the conversation went from somewhat warm to extremely warm and personable, immediately.

Another time I was on the phone with a past client, and I asked them how their daughter was doing at the university she was attending. We talked about that for a little while. When the conversation stalled, I asked them if they ever got that promotion that they'd hoped to get.

I had taken a long note about this specifically, because they were really counting on that promotion to improve their lives at the time. He did get the promotion and was currently in the process of working toward another one. The conversation flowed smoothly from there.

Note in these two stories that there was no way I would have remembered those details without my CRM. The rapport I was able to build with these two people based on remembering things important to them was extremely valuable. And, as I always suggest, keeping the conversation centered around them made our call much less about business and more about friendship.

One easy way of using these details for quick laid-back contact with people in your database is sending them a quick text in response to something you know they follow. For example, I have a client who's a big Kansas City Chiefs fan. When I see that the Chiefs have won a game or I come across a headline about the team making a trade, I will send him a text in reference to that: "Congrats on the win yesterday" or "I can't believe they traded so-and-so." These texts are very well-received by people because they love talking sports with their friends.

Implementing the Strategy

Now that you have some examples of why this is important, let's start implementing this strategy in your business.

- Look over your names in your CRM. What information do you have about your clients? Do you need to add advanced information about any of them?

- The first step to finding this information is to brainstorm about your previous conversations with them. Do not discount simple information. It can be as simple as, "They used to live in Los Angeles, and now they live in San Francisco." After you have taken down notes on everything, you can form conversations, visit Facebook, and click on the About tab, which should have a list of their favorite TV shows, sports teams, etc. If you can't get information there, you may find some of their posts on Instagram or Twitter. Some 99% of people will have information available somewhere. It's your job to find it and put it in your CRM. If all else fails, and with that remaining 1%, you will be building this information from scratch based on your phone calls and interactions with them.

- Pick at least five clients and add advanced information: hobbies, spouse's name, children's names, favorite sports teams, what college did they attend? Where do they work? Because you are only doing five names, make it a goal to enter at least 10 data points for each name.

- The best place to start is with people who will likely be buying or selling soon. With that in mind, pull the top five names from your Money List and begin there. If you want to do more than five over the next several days, complete every name on your Money List before moving on to the rest of your database.

- It is important that you are in front of your people frequently. This can be via personal contacts, advertising, or interactions on social media. You want them to feel that you care about them.

- It is impossible to be in constant contact with everybody in your database. For this reason, sit down with your coach and strategize about other methods to make sure that you are staying in front of your clients.

- Set reminders in your Google Calendar or some other method for each of five people, for a date to contact them. If your CRM has the capability, as Google does, make it repeat however many times is appropriate.

For example, if someone belonged on my A list in my CRM, I would set a reminder to personally contact them monthly.

- Make it a goal to contact at least five people today or tomorrow, and use the information you were able to gather to hopefully have a better conversation next time. Be careful not to rattle off what you know, and don't make it obvious that you have been doing your research. If nothing comes up organically, you can say, "Hey, I saw on Facebook that you're a Packers fan. How did that happen?" This specifically came up in a conversation with a friend of mine. I asked him this question when the conversation stalled a little bit, and the story of how he became a Packers fan was funny. His uncle had given him a pair of Packers socks when he was 8 years old, and he started following the team from there. I took note in my CRM that if I ever sold him a house, in addition to any gift I gave him at closing, I would also give him a pair of Packers socks. The moral of the story: It expanded our conversation by five minutes, and we were able to have a few laughs together. I will likely use this strategy listed above by texting him every now and again about the team when they have big wins or interesting trades. This is a very easy way for me to keep in touch with him.

With these methods, you will be building true, longer relationships that will result in repeat business and referrals. You will likely enjoy your day-to-day work because you will become a relationship manager and a friend, rather than just a salesman. This will make it so that cold calls and other lead-generating methods will become optional rather than required in the long run.

Conclusion

The old adage, as corny as it may be, still holds to be true:

People don't care how much you know, until they know how much you care.

Translated into real estate or other sales, everybody has at least ten options, and some of those options are related to them and tied to some sort of emotional obligation. The only way to overcome the competition is to add the X Factor of friendship. Expanding your database of close friends from five or ten people to dozens and dozens of people, will ensure steady business and exponential growth for years to come.

Chapter 22

Creativity in Client Relationship-Building

The more people feel appreciated and taken care of, the stronger your relationship with them. And that will naturally result in more business for you. We will teach you how customer appreciation events can grow your business by strengthening your relationships with clients.

Fun events, such as movie nights or themed dinners, can create an experience that is memorable for your clients and friends.

Such events are great for building relationships with clients, and for raising your profile in the community.

Not only will people who attend have a deeper relationship with you, but even the people you invite, but who could not make it, really appreciate the gesture of your setting up the event and inviting them to it.

Movie Nights

We have done many kinds of events over the years. I would have to say our most successful events have been movie nights. Why? Because they require very little preparation and the cost is minimal. For this reason, we have been able to do them frequently. They're cost-effective, too, because you can talk to vendors about sharing the expenses.

At a recent movie event, I invited about two hundred people. I stood at the door greeting everybody, missing the beginning of the movie (as usual), and with about a ten-minute gap of nobody arriving, I went inside to watch the movie. A few minutes later, I realized that I had forgotten my popcorn and went out to get it.

Thank goodness I did that, because waiting next to the popcorn stand was one of my friends (and later client) whom I had invited. He had arrived super late. We were able to have a great quick interaction as we moved into the theater, and it led to a phone call later that evening. Turns out he was about to enter into an agreement with another agent in my specialty area.

Despite my frequent Facebook posts, and the fact that I had been in touch with him a few times a year, he had forgotten to contact me at the beginning of the process. Even more surprising, he likely would have attended the event and still used the other REALTOR® if I had not had the face-to-face interaction with him.

Within two weeks, he was under contract on a $900,000 house, one of my biggest commissions of the year.

Before he got to the event, as people were filing into their seats, I walked around passing out candy bars in exchange for people correctly answering trivia questions about the movie. One of my great past clients, Angie, was super excited to win a Snickers bar. Whether it was because I had a quick, fun verbal exchange with her there, or the movie itself, I will never know. But I received a referral from her that evening for her neighbor who was selling a house.

It's important to remember that if you were to buy leads like this they would cost well over $1,000, because the rate of conversion is so high. The fact is, one referral from a movie night can pay for the event five times over.

However, it's also important to never do these events solely for the purpose of collecting leads. As you work the program, you'll generate leads, but keep in mind that some of these events are simply to thank current and past clients. When you have the right mindset, and the people attending your event can feel that you truly appreciate them, then the value of the event will be much higher than any immediate financial results.

While major events are important, and preferably done quarterly, make sure that you arrange smaller gatherings on at least a monthly business. These can be intimate seminars, but preferably a party at your house or a dinner of some kind.

Early in my career for one of those events, I agreed to host a bachelor party at my house. It was not a huge commitment, because everybody who came was pretty laid back and there was no alcohol involved. We ended up playing cards for about three or four hours. Only two people attended that I didn't know, but I had extended conversations with each of them.

The value in these small events is that you are able to spend more time with individuals, whereas in a large event you cannot. I got to know both of those unknown people I had met there really well and added them to my database. It is no surprise that I am currently helping one of them buy a house.

Seminars, on the other hand, require a lot more advertising because not everyone is interested in the topic.

At a recent seminar, I invited a friend of mine and was surprised he came because it was in regard to investing in Utah real estate. He only invests in Florida, but he wanted to come and learn a little bit more about investment strategies for Utah. After the seminar was over, we sat and chatted for an additional 30 minutes.

It turns out that I was not only able to find out that he was looking for a new agent in Florida (which gave me the opportunity to help him find one and collect a referral fee), but we were also able to explore why Utah is a great market for investment properties, as well.

Putting Together an Event

Here's how to make sure you've got all the bases covered when you put together a client event:

- If you have closed many transactions in the past, review the list of people whom you have used as home inspectors, as insurance agents, as a home warranty specialist, or any other industry you feel might be likely to contribute to the event. I even had a photographer participate in one of my events, because he knew if I got a new listing he would get a job taking the photos for the listing.

- Call each of them and see who is willing to financially contribute or contribute something else of value, such as organizing the event or working on getting discounts from the venue.

- Call a meeting before the event and have all the vendors who will be participating attend. At this meeting, you will set the metrics for organizing your client event.

- Make sure everything is assigned so that the event will run smoothly, and that everyone knows that they are expected to be there at least an hour before the event. You want to make sure that everyone will be collaborating so that everything runs smoothly.

- Some things to assign:
  - If you don't have an events manager, you need one who knows how to create/ assign an events team, such as a team like the following:
  - Someone to plan the event.

- Someone to find the venue.
- Another to set the date.
- Someone experienced to determine the menu.
- Someone to design and distribute the invitations (email, paper, text, online).
- Have yet another set parameters: running time, starting time, ending time.
- Someone to set, manage, and allocate the budget.
- You need someone standing at a table to collect tickets or hand out something of value (such as gift bags).
- Someone to organize the event with the venue and to help pick the best spots to have people stationed at.
- If food is involved, someone can be in charge of picking out great food and making sure it is delivered promptly and put in the right place.
- Put someone in charge of gathering leads and information and finding a discreet and non-intrusive way to do so.
- You can have a colleague or vendor be the one to invite people. Make sure they are reminded about the event at least four times before the event.
- You will also want someone to be in charge of follow-ups after the event.

- If you're doing a seminar or something that requires additional preparation, you need to ask yourself beforehand,
  - What is the subject? For example, are you teaching a class on how to get the most out of your home when selling it? How to be a successful buyer or, perhaps, how to invest in real estate?
  - Depending on what the subject is, you need to determine who will speak. It could be a local expert of some kind, someone from your office, a satisfied client. Just make sure that you have the floor at some point and preferably you will teach many classes in their entirety, with guest speakers to chime in every now and then.

- Now you are ready to hold an event. Use a CRM to make a list of people you would like to invite, starting, of course, with the A's.

- Make lists of invitees.

Ask yourself these questions

- How will the event be organized?

- How will you interact with prospects and clients? Brainstorm with your team on the best way to do this.

- Make written notes of all details for each event, identifying specific goal(s) for each.

Thanks to these events, your clients and friends will feel appreciated, and they will leave the event feeling you have no ulterior motive. I would hope that this is absolutely true. There's a reason they call them customer-appreciation events.

And referrals and more business will be a natural result of your genuine appreciation.

Conclusion

When you run these events correctly, and you make sure to have at least a short personal interaction with each person who attends, you will be able to strengthen dozens of relationships in one night. If you are successful and people leave feeling truly appreciated—and that you have no ulterior motives—the strength of these friendships will expand, and referrals will undoubtedly follow.

Chapter 23

The Process Leading Up to Closing

Have you ever dropped the ball on a transaction?

Has your client ever called you and asked you for an update? Have your clients ever expressed frustration, either verbally or nonverbally, indicating that they do not feel you are doing enough? We have all been there.

In this chapter, we will teach you how never to have those things happen again, and also to create the complete opposite effect, where no matter how good or bad a transaction goes, your clients will see you as a professional and an advocate for them.

The big idea here is that during the process of working with a client, from the beginning stages of a consultation to the contract and eventual closing, you will have an opportunity to turn them into raving fans. This is the difference between a single closed transaction and an amazing referral partner who could potentially give you three or four referrals every single year.

A Demanding Client

One client I had early in my career was particularly demanding. I was grateful for this later on after I realized he had helped show me how to take care of clients when they have very specific needs.

He specifically wanted frequent updates, regardless of whether there was anything new or not. For instance, we might have no phone calls, no showings or updates on advertising, but he still wanted me to text and let him know that there was nothing new.

Sometimes it was as simple as a text that said, "No update today — any questions?"

More often than not, he had no questions, but he wanted that ongoing contact. Suffice to say, during the process of helping him sell his home, we spoke every day for nearly two months. Obviously, our relationship grew much more rapidly than with other clients because of the frequency of communication, but he also felt that I did more for him than any other salesman he had ever worked with.

I was committed to him and willing to be on top of the process 100% of the time. And he truly appreciated that.

This man held a high-level position at his company, and I was just starting out as an agent. And it showed. I had low-quality clothing and even wore ratty tennis shoes rather than dress shoes when I met with him. While I recommend presenting yourself better than I had, the point is that the level of customer service I provided was able to outshine every other aspect of the process. His referrals have generated over 10% of my sales every year since that time. Most recently, he referred me to four transactions within a two-month period, one of which quoted back to me what he had told them: "Call Brian. You're an idiot if you go with anybody else."

This client was able to teach me that, regardless of whether your future clients want a call every day or not, you need to review their files daily and update them frequently. This has enabled me to solve problems and avoid mistakes with my clients over the years. The result is, my clients have grown into raving fans rather than just neutral players in yet another closed transaction.

Here are several examples of how you can stay on top of the

process of taking care of your client. For instance, when you are listing a home, call the buyer's lender and the buyer's agent frequently throughout the transaction. When I've done this, it has helped me avoid mistakes that they would have made, based on forgetting or not doing a good job of keeping up on the details in their notes about the transaction.
A specific example of the need to do this comes from an agent I was coaching, who had a home under contract. He did a great job contacting his client throughout the process, but he did not actually contact other people involved in the transaction to make sure it went smoothly on their end.

It turned out that the buyer's real estate agent never notified the loan company that the home was under contract. It was not until one week before closing that the contract made it to the loan officer, which caused a thirty-day extension. This created a lot of hardship for the seller, but greater catastrophe followed when the buyers fell victim to fraud in something else and lost their down payment.

At this point, the transaction had been running for nearly a hundred days, and the home had to go back on the market. If the buyer's REALTOR® had simply called the selling agent and called the lender within the first week, the home likely would have closed on time, saving his client from a lot of frustration and the buyer from losing their life savings to fraud.

When you take care of the process and make the client feel that you are there for them all the time, you will truly separate yourself from the pack of average REALTORS®.

When you do this, you can even gain referrals when the results with the current clients are not optimal. For instance, I listed a for-sale-by-owner that sat on the market for nearly six months. We only had a handful of showings, and no offers. The owners ended up taking the home off the market, but a couple of weeks after that, they referred me to their mother, whom I was able to help complete a real estate transaction.

I asked them, when I thanked them for the referral, why they had referred their mother to me. They told me they had been so impressed by my constant communication, and they could tell I had been doing everything in my power to sell their home.

It didn't matter that we had not been successful. At the end of the day, the constant communication and my level of care helped them feel comfortable referring me to their own mother because they knew she would be in good hands.

Now that you have a better understanding of how to take great care of clients, let's build your pipeline for current clients. Here's how:

- Review your Money List. Begin with your 0's (your active clients), specifically, homes you already have under contract or listed.

- Note where these people are in the process. Are they new clients, close to closing, etc.? You want to know where each of them is in the process because the messaging differs for each stage of the process.

    - If you need to send follow-up emails, do this now. If you need to return a call or text to one of these current clients, do it now. This is important because, before you go out looking for new business, you need to take care of your current clients.

    - Before you make calls, and during them, if you have not already done so, ask your clients how often they want updates, and how they would prefer to receive those updates. Try also to observe their individual needs and preferences.

- Once you have caught up on all of your current clients, it's time to start calling or texting everyone on the 1, 2, 3 list, starting now with the 1's. It is important to note that, before and during these calls, you should take great notes.

- Once you have completed this (and it may take several days), you will also want to review your CRM. As you make phone calls to people on your CRM, think about things you can have a conversation with them about that will build the relationship. Is there anything non-business related you can discuss? Wedding anniversary? Birthday? Sporting events, etc.?

- For current clients, if any specific milestones are coming up in the transaction — for example, offer accepted, financing and appraisal deadline passed, or home put on the market — consider getting them a small gift or gift card and sending it out today. You can also do this with birthdays or anniversaries or personal milestones if there's nothing in the transaction that merits some sort of card or acknowledgement. Do not get hung up on the hassle of buying a gift card and labeling an envelope. If you are not likely to do this, send them a digital gift card. You can do that while you are on the phone with them. For example, "That's so great that your anniversary is coming up. I want to send you a quick little gift card. Where do you guys like to go out to eat?"

- Now that you are up to date on all of your current clients, you need to spend as much time as possible creating a foolproof stay-on-top process. The goal is to stay on top of things so that you never drop the ball for these clients again. Google Search or ask your coach for a listing checklist and a buyer's checklist.

- Do not simply use these lists as is. It is your job to make them exhaustingly comprehensive. For instance, a buyer's list that you get online might have these bullet points to do before you go see a home for them:

    1. Have an initial buyer consultation.

    2. Sign buyer-broker agreement.

3. Set up automatic hot sheets.

- Your to-do list needs to look different from this. Yours will say something more like:

    1. Schedule initial consultation.
    2. Research people on Facebook and see what an appropriate gift would be to give them at that consultation.
    3. Send follow-up text reminding them of the upcoming meeting.
    4. Bring the gift to the buyer's consultation, with a card attached.
    5. Set them up on automatic hot sheets.
    6. Send a thank-you text that evening after your consultation. This text should thank them for trusting you as their REALTOR® and promising them great customer service.
    7. Follow up the next day after sending them properties and see what they liked and did not like about the properties they receive.
    8. Adjust the hot sheets according to their feedback.

- You get the idea. A great buyer's checklist will include not only essential items to be done, but gives reminders for frequent communication. I would not be surprised if this checklist includes more than 50 bullet points.

- Obviously, your list is much more detailed and comprehensive than any generic ones you found online. Use these generic lists only as a framework for building your own. After you have made this list, it may be discouraging to look at all these items. You may ask yourself: How will I have time for all these things? The answer is simple: If you do all of the items in these checklists, you will likely not need to spend time on advertising or making cold calls, because these clients will provide you with your next wave of business, via referrals.

If you have followed the advice in this and in previous chapters, these clients are probably already good friends. They will realize that not only are you a fantastic friend, but you are also an extremely skilled REALTOR®. At this point, it will become a no-brainer decision to refer you to their friends and family. These two things in combination (your friendship and your amazing service during the transaction) will become an unstoppable force for referrals.

Conclusion

When you follow a detailed sales process and you take possession of the transaction to the point of excessive communication and relentless protection of your client and their needs, your efforts will shine brightly to your clients, and your transactions will go much more smoothly. This will result in future loyalty and unlimited referrals.

Never forget that your current clients know enough people to generate over 100 referrals per year. If you can just tap into 2% or 3% of these potential referrals, each of your transactions should generate two to three additional transactions. Can you imagine the compound effect this will create?

Chapter 24

Closing and Client Work

Each of your real estate transactions has the potential to turn into an additional two to three transactions within the next year — that is, if you follow your checklist with each client and allow them to see how hard you are working for them. Then they will feel you are taking great care of them. Your clients will be happy with you, and your real estate business will grow quickly.

Through using the right process, you can create an atmosphere within each transaction so your clients feel extremely comfortable and grateful to you for what you do for them. When this happens, your income and sales will increase with a compound effect.

Unfortunately, I learned the hard way about the necessity for being on top of my game in a closing. It was one of my first transactions. My mentor threw the ball in my court and had me lead the closing, although I had only completed two sales prior to this one. And this was, in fact, my very first listing.

Knowing what I know now, thinking of somebody completing an entire transaction for their first time without any help is terrifying. I am lucky I didn't repeat the errors I made in that instance.

No Seller's Checklist

My clients were an elderly couple, and they were selling their home of twenty years in order to afford a retirement home out of state. They knew exactly how much they needed from selling their home to retire. And they would either not sell if they couldn't get that amount, or they would have to find a part-time job at their new location in Arizona. I called them about once a week throughout the process. We got it under contract, and then it fell through.
Before I get into what went wrong, I did something right, luckily, to make this sale happen. When the first contract was cancelled, they decided to take their home off the market and try again next year. However, I still felt that I had not completed my job for them, so I continued following up with all the REALTORS® who had shown the home. About two months later, one of them took the bait and brought their clients back over. We put it back on the market, and it sold immediately to that buyer.

At that time, I did not have as detailed of a seller's checklist as I do now. The specific item I wish I had was sending the clients the closing document and reviewing it with them prior to closing, or even better, prior to them accepting the offer.

In this instance, I did a good job (but not a great job) of letting them know what to expect. We even did some math over the phone, and I told them what they'd be walking away with, down to within $100. But when the title officer came to their home and sat down for closing, my sweet client put her hand to her mouth in shock when she saw the amount they would be getting.

Her husband turned to her and said, "I told you so."

It was one of the most awkward moments of my career. The title officer shifted in his seat, I was uncomfortable, and my client was on the verge of tears as her husband bitterly said, "I told you so."

Unfortunately, I was still pretty green and wanted to jump in and defend myself. Granted, I made an offering at first to try and ease the situation. I was only at a 1.5% commission, but I said, "Is there anything I can do to make this hurt a little bit less?" They were good people and knew how hard I had worked on their deal. He said no, and she agreed.

After that, due to my lack of experience, I made the mistake of reminding him, "Do you remember me calling you and going over these numbers?" Yes, he said, adding that he had tried to tell his wife and that she probably hadn't listened to him. Tension was continuing to rise, and she was getting more and more emotional as he continued to belittle her forgetfulness.

Long story short, they ended up signing the document, shaking my hand, and everybody went about their lives.

They called me three days later to thank me for everything I had done. He told me, "Can I give you some tips for your career? I know how hard you work, and I want you to be successful." I welcome correction when it is direct and well intended, so I eagerly agreed to hear his advice. He told me that I needed to have better communication after a home went under contract.

I did not ask, and I'll never know, but there is a good chance that, due to his age, he may have completely forgotten the conversation where I told him how much he would end up walking away with. This hurt the most because I felt that one of them did not feel they were misled. But I had to wonder if he also felt that they were never told how much money they would walk away with before they committed to the sale.

Fast forward to when I had a more extensive seller checklist. This time I did what I recommend for everybody to do — I brought a second agent in on the transaction. By the way, if you choose to do joint transactions with other agents, it is essential that you build up this agent with your clients; do not call them an assistant or one of your team members. Call them a member of the team or a colleague, so that the client can trust them.

From the day we listed the house to the day it closed, we had a joint text thread going between him, his wife, myself, and the agent I had brought in on the deal. Because there were two of us working the deal, the clients were contacted at least once daily. The text thread often would have five or ten new messages in it, before I even looked at my phone. They were getting quick responses from my teammate because he was new in the industry, and they were his only clients at the time.

I was managing those responses and continually training him on best practices. When an offer came, in contrast to the previous story, we had the title company draw up an estimated settlement statement before my seller even made a decision on whether or not to accept the offer.

Their final walk-away amount was within $100 of what they were expecting, and we reviewed the settlement statement with them once before they accepted the offer, and again three days before closing, and again the night before closing.

Closing can be long, drawn-out, and awkward, especially when there are terrible surprises, as in the story I shared earlier of the elderly couple.

I have sat in the closing room for over an hour as a client has sifted through every item and asked question after question. It can get awkward and often hostile when they come across things they somehow hadn't noticed before.

When you review everything in advance (preferably in person), signing can sometimes take as little as five or 10 minutes, which gives you half an hour to an hour to shoot the breeze, strengthen the relationship, and congratulate them on the completion of the sale.

In the second story, I received two referrals within a week of closing. I have no doubt I will receive several every year moving forward if I manage all my closings as well as that one.

Best Practices

In the previous chapter, we went over best practices you should follow during the listing period. Here we will review how, as a result of doing these best practices, you will be able to generate referrals.

First, however much you were communicating before with your clients, you absolutely have to double and triple your communication to the point where you are in touch with them a minimum of every other day.

There are many different types of sellers. Some want to know whenever there's an update. But others want only to know if something terrible happens, and they couldn't care less to have frequent updates about anything less than that.

I have found , however, that the second person described is not bothered by an email or a text with an update. For this reason, every time there is a new update in a transaction, at the very minimum I send them a text or email even if it is several in one day. For example, "I just spoke to the loan officer. He said the buyers were moving along well." Or "I spoke to the other agent. He said the buyer is still excited about the house." Or "The inspection is scheduled for Tuesday. Is there anything you want to do before that?" Or "I spoke with the loan company. I will let you know when I get the exact time and date for closing." These are just some sample texts you could send for frequent updates.

The four examples listed above serve two purposes. First, if your client is like most people, they want to know what's happening because they are desperately scared of the deal falling apart.

But even if they are the second seller we described, who does not care for an update unless the home is falling out of contract, this will ensure that they see that you are doing your job.

The public perception is that a real estate agent puts a home under contract, waits a month, and then gets paid an unfair commission. You need to change this perception in your seller's mind so that they pay you a full commission next time you work with them and refer you to others. Remember, over-communicating is infinitely better than under-communicating.

Checklist

Make sure every time you do a checklist with the seller that you check it off with a pen or pencil. This will give you satisfaction, make you work harder, and help you continue to increase your productivity. I would also recommend when you are filling out your to-do list on your yellow pad that you add these items to it daily. This will give you another reminder to do the items on your checklist. But you also have to write it down rather than simply checking it off a list you print out.

If you are not a computer person, get a new folder for all of your clients and insert this to-do list in the folder with their name at the top.

Look at your to-do list several times a day. If you are a computer person, you can use a to-do list app, if you choose. But it is my opinion, physically checking it off with a pen or pencil gives you more of a feeling of accomplishment, especially for those of us who did not grow up with an electronic tablet in our hand.

As you move through the transaction, ask your client at least once a week how things are going. Sample questions: "Is there anything else I can do to make you feel good about how the transaction is proceeding" or "Do you have any concerns right now" or "Have I done anything you're not happy with up to this point? I want to make sure I'm taking great care of you. So, please be honest and don't worry about offending me." These questions will help you improve your process and allow your client to feel valued and heard.

Don't be shy. Over the course of my coaching career, I have heard this about a hundred times: "I'm not good about asking for referrals" or "I don't like asking for referrals."

Listen carefully: If you are doing your job right, your clients want to give you referrals!

They are just waiting for you to remind them to do it.

Referrals Aren't Automatic

Believe it or not, some clients don't even know whether you'd accept a referral.

They might see how busy you are and don't think you have time, or they have a friend in Texas and don't know that you could refer an agent in another state and collect a referral fee. Every time I work with clients and check off each of the 50 or so items on the to-do list, they have eagerly accepted the challenge of finding me a referral.

Here are some good examples of ways to ask the questions that are not pushy: "Hey, now that we have passed the due diligence deadline, there is less for me to worry about within your transaction, which means I have some time on my hands. Have you spoken to anyone recently who has mentioned buying or selling real estate that you could refer me to? I would like to stay busy and don't mind making money, either, hah-hah." Or "I hope I've taken good enough care of you at this point that you would feel comfortable referring me to friends and family. My team is taking on new clients, and we have an opening for two or three new clients right now. Has anyone you know mentioned lately that they're moving?"

When you ask these questions, your clients will likely say one of two things:

A: "Actually, yeah, my cousin Jimmy was talking about this, and said they were thinking about moving in six months." (It's important to tell them that even six to eight months out you would love the referral right now and make the contact.) I would love to connect you to him."

Or B: "I haven't really met anyone lately buying or selling, but I will definitely keep you in mind."

Here are the responses you can give these clients:

For Client A, you will say, "That's fantastic! Could you give me his phone number or start a joint text thread so I could introduce myself?" If he simply wants to give his friend your phone number, I have found they only call you about 10% to 20% of the time.

However, if you get the phone number, your chances of becoming the agent on that transaction increase to 50% or 60%. These percentages might seem low to you, but remember that often this referral is coming to you after they have already seen homes with another agent or perhaps are thinking of working with a family member who is a REALTOR®.

For Client B, the best reaction is, "That's great! I would absolutely love for you to keep me in mind. Don't forget, I can help out-of-state buyers as well as buyers here." These two examples should not come across as pushy. If they hesitate to give you a phone number, let it go quickly. Don't push too hard, but let them know why you need it.

Because my clients have become such good friends, I do not hesitate to share statistics about how infrequently people actually end up calling me, and how much better it is for me to contact them. If they hesitate to give me the number, I encourage them to ask their friends if they'd be comfortable with them sharing their phone number with me. I will then call my client a few days later and ask if their friend had agreed to give me their phone number.

Don't be afraid to ask for referrals on a commission that could be as high as $15,000 or more. Imagine what you might be missing out on if you do not at least try.

REALTORS® can do so well in the contract process that their client will not only be extremely happy and satisfied, but they will be champing at the bit to refer you to their friends. They may even look at it as an opportunity to strengthen their relationship with their friends by extending you as a resource to them.

Conclusion

Your current clients will become raving fans and satisfied customers when you do everything described in this chapter. And as an added benefit, you will likely never get sued or even have to go to mediation. Remember, always be honest, and always communicate quickly and frequently. As you do this and ask for referrals, your clients will gladly help you grow your real estate business by giving referrals to you.

Chapter 25

How to Manage Transactions with Friends and Family

Sometimes real estate relationships are confusing, because being someone's good friend, as well as a trusted and respected advisor, is a delicate balance.

I have found that the best way to achieve success in this balance is to be extremely honest and show tough love to clients when needed.

Most of your friends will not tell you things you do not want to hear. Having fun and joking around and then immediately telling them about a serious situation is no problem at all, as long as you sound extremely confident, knowledgeable, and you are clear about the direction that you advise them to go in.

Real estate will improve your current relationships as long as you have a gameplan on how to handle the delicate balance of friendship and business.

When you handle it correctly, your job will likely become very fun, while simultaneously making you a lot of money.

Friends as Clients

An example of this concept is Liam and his wife, Laura. I had sold them a house a couple of years prior after having met them at a dinner party. They decided they wanted to upgrade their home, so I met them to show them a couple of properties.

As we walked toward the home from our parking space, we laughed about several inside jokes, and I had a great time. When we arrived at the house, I immediately switched into my professional mode and started telling them about the features of the home and pointing out any problems I saw.
This flowed naturally because, although we had become great friends, they had a ton of respect for me as a REALTOR®.

So, seeing those two sides of me one right after the other did not seem awkward at all. And they actually did the same thing and started acting like clients again. After we went over the features of the home, we then started laughing and joking again. It came as no surprise to me that before we even went under contract on a property, they sent me a referral.

In this case, I didn't even ask, but I had asked in the past, so they knew I was always looking for referrals.

Getting Better

Let's review what you have done in the past so that we can improve your future conduct with friends and family, your Sphere of Influence.

If you have sold a home to a friend or a family member, try to go back in your mind and think of how you handled difficult situations, how you interacted with them, and how the relationship either improved or deteriorated by the end of the process.

Were they satisfied? Did they feel that you took great care of them? Or does part of you wonder whether they regretted working with you and that they may be thinking of not doing it again?

Now that you have gone back and explored past experiences, take out a sheet of paper and write down each negative item that happened during those transactions. If you have done dozens of transactions with friends and family, be selective and don't take up anything like an hour in doing this. So maybe focus on one or two of the most unpleasant transactions.

After writing down each item that negatively impacted your client relationships in the past, create something you can put in your future checklist that will prevent such things from happening. This is also a great time to remind yourself why you do what you do (your what-why) and recognize how important these people are to you. Damaging your relationships with these people based on making a living is exactly why many REALTORS® feel the need to quit. You do not need to quit — you just need to fix some problems.

If you are currently working with any friends or family, or you plan to do so within the next several months, open up your CRM and review any past notes about them, their hobbies, family situation, job situations, etc. If your CRM is not yet that detailed, open up their Facebook or Instagram page and refamiliarize yourself with their life.

As silly as it may sound, play out some conversations you may have with them during the process about casual or fun things, such as talking about a favorite TV show you both like. These are the types of conversations that will help the relationship stay a friendship and help you avoid staying simply a REALTOR®.

Interestingly, according to a study by the folks behind the book *Ninja Selling*, only 40% of real estate agents have some semblance of a database. On average, those with databases earn over 251% more income than the 60% without a database. That's worth noting, right?

Remember, it is absolutely essential that while joking around and having fun is important, these people need to see you as a professional they respect and trust. You need to put strong, conscious effort into creating a perfect balance that will breed good experiences and referrals, as well as good friends.

When you work on improving how you conduct your transactions with your Sphere of Influence, your friends and family will appreciate you not only as a good buddy, but also as a trusted professional. In the optimal world of real estate business we're all hoping to create, selling somebody a house will actually strengthen the bond in your friendship, while simultaneously impressing them and giving them more trust in you as a professional.

Conclusion

Your friends and family are likely already the lifeblood of your real estate business. If they are not, they are the easiest group of people to become so. Creating the perfect balance between friendship and professionalism will ensure that they feel comfortable with you, happy with you, and will refer you to others consistently.

Now, there's a cornucopia worth cultivating!

Chapter 26

You've Closed — What's Next?

Now that your clients have had a fantastic experience with you, and you've handled closing day on their property of choice correctly, the fun work begins.

If you are consistent with great post-transaction care for the next twelve months, your efforts should result in a minimum of one referral per closing. Actually, though, using our methods fully and conscientiously, each of your closings will result in at least two referrals per closing. Here you will read about an agent who discovered the value of proper post-transaction care, which increased his referrals dramatically.

The big idea is that when you turn your clients into raving fans, your income can triple every year. If you continue to do this throughout your career, your database of raving fans will be producing so many referrals that you will likely need to hire several employees or maybe even start a team just to handle your own personal production.

There are shocking statistics out there about REALTOR® agents who do not follow up with past clients, as compiled in the book *Ninja Selling* by Larry Kendall. When home sellers were asked if they use the same REALTOR® again, 84% said they would. But on the next transaction, only 25% of them actually did. Similarly, when buyers were asked the same question, 88% of them responded that they would use the same REALTOR® on their next transaction, but only 12% did. This proves the importance of follow-up and post-transaction care. I will tell you two stories about an agent named Shiloh to illustrate the importance of following up after closings.

A Story of Referrals

I was training Shiloh early in his career. He had closed over 100 transactions. We laid out his business plan and found that he had only received four referrals in his career from past clients. He seemed to think this was acceptable and wanted advice on cold calling and how to work the FSBO (For-Sale-By-Owner) market. When I told him those hundred sales should have resulted in two hundred more sales, he scoffed audibly.

As we worked together on the plan described below, he started to see a referral out of every two or three clients, on average. Obviously, these results were not optimal, and our continuous goal was to get at least two referrals from every client. But it was a good start.

It will come as no surprise to you that after Shiloh began to receive referrals from past clients more consistently, he was very disappointed to realize that of his first hundred-plus transactions, he could have sold a minimum of an extra thirty homes even just according to his statistics at that time, which have drastically improved since then.

Let's move on to the first time Shiloh asked for a referral. He and I wrestled over it for two or three phone calls. He didn't want to do it. Finally, he was at the closing table (it's much better to do it at least once prior to closing). He told his clients that he'd love to work with any of their friends and family. Knowing Shiloh, I doubt he made eye contact when he asked. They happily referred him to their brother and sister-in-law. Shiloh made an additional $11,000 on that sale, and I believe that, if he had spent the hours cold-calling that he spent working with that referral, he may have made the same amount of money. But the experience would have been much more exhausting.

Today, his business is built almost entirely on referrals. He ended up becoming proficient at cold-calling, and he now does it as a hobby when he has a little bit of spare time between clients.

Shiloh worked a little differently about a year later.

He handled his closing transaction masterfully, checking off every item on his buyer to-do list.

Of course, as a result of this, his buyers were absolutely thrilled with the experience. When he went into post-transaction care, he had already set himself up for success because his clients considered him the best REALTOR® out there, and now he just had to build the relationship.

His client, Rob, and he developed a particularly close bond. They would interact frequently via text and had several inside jokes. I instructed Shiloh to spend downtime at open houses calling his Sphere of Influence. One day he was doing an open house, and he decided to give Rob a call. Thank goodness no visitors came for quite a while, because it ended up being a one-hour and twenty-minute conversation between him and Rob!

A couple of weeks later, he got a phone call from one of Rob's friends. Over the course of the conversation, Shiloh asked him what Rob said, because most people don't actually call when they are referred to a REALTOR®. He said that Rob had been pestering him literally for months. Every time the topic of buying a house would come up, he would say something like, "You got to use Shiloh. C'mon, you know you want to use Shiloh. You're not going to use a crappy REALTOR®, are you? Let me give you Shiloh's phone number."

After the client consultation, Shiloh called Rob to thank him for the referral and to see what gift card he wanted. During the process of thanking him, they had a good laugh when Rob said, "I was just as on top of getting you that referral as you were on top of getting us this house."

If that's not a raving fan, I don't know who is.

Beyond Closing

Here is how to cultivate clients beyond the closing:

- Where will your post-closing referrals come from? There are three sources of referrals after a transaction.
    - First, your client is the treasure trove, the biggest resource.
    - Second, the loan officer, regardless of whether you're helping the buyer or the seller.
    - Third (but much less likely), the title officer.
- Start with your clients.

  It is essential that the client you've just helped become a part of your A's list in your CRM. This means they are receiving something from you four times a month or at least seeing your face four times a month, even if it is primarily via advertising. Make sure one of those four times is in-person or a physical reminder, such as a letter or a phone call.

  I would say that these people almost qualify as an A+ category, because they already know how great it is to work with you, unlike others on your A's list who haven't actually used you yet. For this reason, I recommend being a little more extravagant. Perhaps check out and arrange for a professional company to do some of your post-transaction client care.

- In order to have extremely effective post-transaction care, it's a good idea to bring a client questionnaire to the closing table. The questionnaire would be something like this:

    - What are the names and ages of your children?
    - When are their birthdays?
    - When is your birthday?
    - When is your wedding anniversary?
    - What are a couple of your favorite movies?
    - What are your favorite sports teams?

  Obviously, the goal of this questionnaire is to give you a head start on filling in the information on your CRM. If you feel this will make them uncomfortable, you may decide to take out the questions about their children. Having items about their children in the questionnaire or not will depend on the level of trust you have built with your client.

  I will often pre-qualify this questionnaire by saying something like, "Could you fill this out? The reason I'm asking for everybody's birthday is because I hope that someday I will be super rich and will be able to send them a gift." I say this with a chuckle, and it usually gets a good laugh from everybody, and they fill it out without hesitation.

  Now that you have this information, here are some ideas for future client contacts:

- Dropping off Christmas gifts; calling them on their birthdays; giving them an anniversary card or perhaps even an anniversary gift. For instance, I will send them each a different gift. I will give the husband a gift card

and say, "Don't forget your wife's anniversary. I don't want you to get in trouble. Hopefully, this helps you get something nice." For the wife, I might send a box of chocolates or something that will not be perceived as romantic, but is an appropriate anniversary gift.
Also, I recommend you do an in-person yearly review of their new property. It should include a new value analysis, names and phone numbers of your preferred vendors for all things home-related (such as plumbers, electricians) and helpful information about different subjects, such as home design, the value of refinancing, or tips and tricks to keep your home's value up with regular maintenance.

  - Just as you did during the closing process, don't forget to ask for referrals, when appropriate. If you follow the scripts provided by us at Diosum Coaching, you should have no problem asking for referrals in a way that is not threatening.

- The second source is loan officers.

  If you are representing the buyer, you probably spoke with the loan officer every two or three days during this process. This probably equates to 15 or more conversations. If you are doing this, you and the loan officer have likely become friends. Most loan officers have a minimum of five referrals to give out to their favorite agents per year. Some loan officers even have that many referrals to give out every month.

  Loan officers are different from clients. You can very easily ask them for referrals whenever you want. They understand the industry and realize that you will likely refer their services to others, as well. Call the loan officer or text them asking for a referral once every two months for up to one year after the transaction closes. Also, consider taking them to lunch at some point during that year.

- Title officers.

  Make sure you do not spend much time on this unless you have completed the first two categories in their entirety. Title officers don't receive more referrals than an average person. But as you will learn, the average person, if they have their eyes and ears open, will hear of about 10 or 20 transactions per year from their own Sphere of Influence.

  Your title officer is much more likely to refer you when asked, because he knows his business depends on your satisfaction with him, and because you will continue to refer him to your clients moving forward. Add your title officer to your database as either a B or an A, depending on how well you got to know them during the closing process. You can ask title officers for referrals maybe once or twice a year.

When agents do all this, they'll stop wasting time on excessive prospecting. And they will start spending their time and money on the machine that will automatically generate referrals faster than they are even able to handle.

Conclusion

Although my strategies and ideology suggest that you may not think of yourself strictly as a salesman, it is important that you realize that great salesmen in other industries do not get results unless they follow up 5 to 7 times.

For this reason, your past clients need to see you several times a month and, hopefully, when they see you they consider it a visit from a friend rather than a sales call. They also need to hear you ask them directly for referrals.

If you have cultivated the relationship well, this won't be an imposition, but a friendly reminder that they will be happy to honor.

Chapter 27

You Can Do This!

After-transaction care is essential to continuing to build strong relationships and obtain referrals. When you do this in combination with continually working your lead sources, you will expand your database exponentially.

When your past clients become your best friends, you cannot wait to start work in the morning, and it's hard to stop at night. You'll enjoy every minute of it, and referrals will flow.

Here's a story of how friends of mine became great clients—

I met Dan and Laurie at a social event. Their sister introduced us, and as we chatted throughout the evening, it came up that I was a REALTOR® and that they were going to be looking for a house later that year. While helping them find a house, we became comfortable with each other. Once the process was over, my wife and I invited them over for dinner. Over the course of the following two years, we attended their daughter's birthday party, they attended our son's birthday party, they had us over to dinner twice, and they attended four or five of my client events.

I would regularly call Dan during open houses when nobody was there, and we would chat about sports and other items of mutual interest. It was no coincidence that they frequently referred me to people, and when it came time for them to buy and sell again (although their next-door neighbor was a REALTOR® who had been courting them and trying to talk them into selling for quite some time), they called me, and we got their home on the market without so much as their interviewing another real estate agent.

Dan and Laueir and their family continue to be some of my very closest friends. This is an example of how, by making your clients into your friends, your business and personal lives are intertwined in the best way.

Keep Adding to Your Database

Now, here's a story of why, despite your best efforts to achieve these positive results, sometimes it will not happen. This shows the need to add new people to your database weekly.

I sold a home to another couple, Tom and Lucy, and took a huge discount on the commission in order to make the purchase work. They were aware of this and seemed to be grateful. As with Dan and Laurie, I continued to cultivate the relationship with Tom and Lucy in a way I felt was very effective. Again, just as happened with Dan and Laurie, when it came time to buy and sell again, they called me without hesitation, and we started to go to work.

This time around, however, because their income had increased and they now had a child, they became much more specific in their preferences. We ended up seeing many, many homes, but they weren't satisfied with any of them.

They grew increasingly frustrated, despite my best efforts to find them a property that worked for them. For example, at one point we saw ten homes in one day. After I added up my costs and the costs of other REALTORS® I paid to help out when I was not available, I was on track to make about $4.50 an hour whenever we would finally close their transaction.

I kept a happy face and continued to treat them as friends. You can imagine my surprise when they ended up buying the house of someone they knew and cut me out completely from the transaction. I was furious, naturally, and technically I could have held them to paying me, thanks to a legally binding document. I called them to ask them why they had done this. They told me they thought I didn't put forth my best effort. They found the home they bought on their own and felt that they didn't have to pay me my commission.

At this point, I realized there were many moments when I should have noticed that they had selfish and narcissistic personalities. After about six months, I felt I could not let go of the friendship, because I felt it had grown strong enough, despite what had happened in that one transaction. So I reached out and took them to lunch. We hashed out what happened, and I cleared up some misconceptions they had about the situation. They kind of apologized, and we continued our relationship.

Then they decided they wanted to buy an investment property. Fool me once . . . . They did the same thing again. And this was after we had gone under contract with them on another home. Because we were already under contract, I had stopped looking for new homes on their behalf, because I thought that this would be unethical when we had a commitment to another seller to go shopping for a different property. They went behind my back to search for homes, despite being under contract. This made me look unprofessional.

Again, they cut me out of the deal and cancelled the contract for the home I had found for them. I called them and, as nicely as possible, I told them what I thought of their way of doing business. I then vowed to myself never to speak with them again. They had referred me to other buyers and sellers a few times, but I felt strongly about not working with them again. Obviously, if I had stopped growing my database, this would have left a hole in my business, which would have meant my business was shrinking rather than expanding.

This experience—choosing to stop doing business with clients I thought were unethical, even though it might have lost me money in the short term—is essential to having integrity in your business.

This motto is not only about how I choose to do business as a REALTOR®, but also whom I choose to do business with. In the end, I have realized that when I turn down business in order to remain ethical and true to my core beliefs, it's actually a good business move, because I remain excited to go to work and because I continue to respect the people I choose to have around me.

Taking Care of Clients

So how do we take care of our clients after a transaction when they do not reach out to us, because they are not in the market to buy or sell a house, and they no longer feel that theyneed our services? Your job is to show them that you can still be a valuable resource, even when they are not buying and selling a home.

- Yearly review.

  A great way to do this is a yearly review. What this looks like is: You take a look at the property you sold your client in the past and do a new comparative market analysis on it. You put this comparative market analysis in a folder, in combination with several other helpful resources about current trends in real estate, local providers of services, and phone numbers that are helpful for hospitals, police departments, schools, etc.

  You will also want to bring a small gift of some kind. Hopefully, if you had them fill out a questionnaire at the closing of the home you sold them, you will have an idea of how to personalize a small gift. For example, it could be as simple as their favorite candy bar.

  - Put this in a neatly organized spiral binder or clipped-together pack and bring it in person. Try to sit down with them for between 15 and 45 minutes, catching up on old times and going over the packet with them.

  - Make sure to end the interview by offering assistance to help with anything and that you're always there to help, happy to receive their phone call.

- Detailed relationship plan.

  In addition to this, you want to make sure you have a detailed relationship plan with each of your clients after their closing. In your CRM, you'll have laid out the frequency of contact, their preferred method of contact, where you see the relationship now, and where you would like to see the relationship go in the future.

  - For example, "Just closed a transaction with Bridget and Weston. I'd like to stay in contact with them once monthly in a personal way, such as a text or phone call. I would also like them to see my advertisement or see a mailer from me once a week on average. I plan on inviting them to several client events and give them a Christmas gift in person.

    Right now, I see the relationship as a trusted adviser and a friend, but not a friend they would necessarily hang out with regularly. I would like to get to the point that they feel comfortable calling me to come over and have a game night. This may or may not happen, but I would like to develop that level of comfort and friendship with them."

- Generating other leads.

  While you were finishing this transaction, you should have been generating other leads from your three pillars of business, which you identified earlier (FSBO, SOI, farming). It is essential that you cultivate current friendships and relationships while simultaneously working your other sources of leads.

- Add weekly to your CRM

  Remember, over the course of your career, hundreds of people will flow in and out of your CRM. It is important to continue adding people weekly to your CRM, or your business transactions will inevitably dry out up some point.

  Become friends.

- The goal here is that all of your previous clients will become your close friends, or they will at least become people who respect and trust you enough to refer you to their friends and family. Remember, your goal is to make work enjoyable for yourself. The best way to do that is to turn all of your clients into good friends. They will love referring you to others, and you will love waking up in the morning and building those new friend-client relationships.

When you have a plan for not only the process, but also for what you will do after the transaction closes, your relationships will be totally in your control, rather than whimsical hopes that never get realized.

Conclusion

Through your systems and goal-setting, you will be able to have closer relationships than otherwise possible, and you will be able to control the direction and the outcome of those relationships in a way that will satisfy everyone, including yourself.

Chapter 28

Your Mindset Makes All the Difference

During the closing process, but especially at the end of a transaction, mindset is everything. It is now time to continue what you have just done to improve your business process, and to follow up frequently. You need to be able to recognize your mistakes during the process in a way that helps you fix them without bringing yourself down or hurting your confidence.

How you approach your life affects how you approach your work. Are you still a victim, are you still entitled? Have you become empowered? This is likely an ever-changing process. And frequent self-evaluation will ensure long-term success.

Here, I'll share a story about Amanda, an agent I worked with who, despite a lot of success, still had a victim mentality.
For instance, on one transaction, she got through 90% of the contract, when the sale inexplicably fell apart at the eleventh hour. It was nothing any of us could have controlled, and I had never seen anything like it in my entire career.

A Victim's Mindset

During our next thirty-minute coaching call after the eleventh hour fiasco just mentioned, Amanda said at least ten things that completely painted her as still having a victim mindset.

Her negative self-talk was extreme and frequent, and I can only imagine that it continued when she got home and vented to her husband. Honestly, I heard it frequently over the next several days via text and email. And we had another phone call where her negative talk dominated most of the conversation again.

On our follow-up coaching call, I asked her what was going on with the couple who had lost that house. "Have you started looking for new properties for them?"

She said she had not contacted them, which made my jaw hit the floor. They were likely as stressed out as she was, and Amanda should have been there for them, comforting them rather than feeling sorry for herself. I told her to get off our call and call them immediately.

When we spoke later, she said that the couple had signed a lease the night before. If she had spoken earlier to them, they would have continued looking for a house with her. But they felt abandoned and were desperate to have somewhere permanent to stay.

With Amanda, it's been an ongoing process to devictimize herself. As part of her upbringing, she was surrounded by other victims. At family get-togethers, the conversation was always about how bad everyone's luck was and how "everyone got screwed by somebody." It's been difficult, but we've made healthy strides in her positive thinking and in her taking ownership for her mistakes. Amanda's sales have increased year over year throughout our client/coach relationship, and she has taken on several roles and responsibilities within her brokerage that would not have been possible with her victim mindset of the past.

Becoming Empowered

With Amanda, we had to use several techniques along the way to help her become empowered. The first time we started one of these exercises was after she was unable to land a client from an open house. She started the same dialogue, telling me

how bad her luck was. I explained to her that how we speak often becomes reality. I instructed her to write down the exact opposite of what she had just told me, twenty-five times a day, until our next call. She ended up sending me a text two days later, telling me how excited she was that she could tell a real difference in her attitude.
Her attitude actually did change. Because she had been telling herself that she was a good salesperson, it made her feel comfortable in pushing past the original rejection from that couple she had met at the open house. She called them one more time to offer her services and explained why she felt she was the right choice. Her text to me was gushing with enthusiasm, as she told me that they were now her clients.

The specific affirmation Amanda had been writing down: "Because I am a great salesperson, people choose to work with me." Try it yourself: twenty-five times a day for a week. It works!

Coasting

Let's visit another story that illustrates the importance of continuing to cultivate business during transactions.

Several years ago, I had the biggest month of my career to that point. In that one month, I closed seven transactions, resulting in $75,000 in commissions. Seven transactions was more than I had ever handled at once. For this reason, I spent all of my time working on those deals. Because of this, I did not work any other lead-generating activities. No cold calls, no SOI calls, no mailers — nothing.

After my wife and I picked up our big paychecks, we went to Disneyland and decided it would be more fun without a budget. Feeling that I had hit the big time, I bought my wife a $15,000 new wedding ring. I also bought a home security system we had been wanting and several other luxuries. I had assumed I would make another $75,000 as easily as I had made the last $75,000.

But I did not.

Looking back, I'm not at all surprised I did not close a single transaction that next month, or the month after that, or the month after that. Not only did I not close another transaction for three months, but because I had spent so much money, we ended up in the hole financially. I had to claw and climb my way out of it.

This is all because I had a terrible mindset as a result of my success — entitlement. I expected new real estate business to just come to me, because, after all, I had done so well for that one month.

This taught me some hard but valuable lessons.

No matter how well you are doing at any given time, you can never stop doing the basics. You have to be continually doing the essential day-to-day tasks that got you where you are now. When you stop doing those things, your real estate transactions will dry up, and when you overspend based on a good month, rather than keep a steady salary for yourself, you will end up running out of money, and this will breed desperation and poor work habits.

Oftentimes, agents with little to no money in their bank account develop what we call "commission breath." Their clients can tell that they need a commission, and they are desperately wanting one in order to survive. It tends to push people away and makes them feel uncomfortable working with you.

My solution to these mistakes was that the next time I had a big month, the only thing my wife and I did differently was go to a nice dinner and celebrate.

The total cost of that dinner and our babysitter was about $250, which was less than 1% of my total income that month. In addition to this, I paid myself only the exact amount I needed to pay my bills that month. The rest of the money went straight into my business savings account. More importantly, as the month progressed, I made sure to make one hour of FSBO calls every morning and keep in touch with my SOI regularly. The following month stayed consistent, and I was able to start building a much more stable business.

How to Make Sure You Don't Get Ahead of Yourself

- Several times during each transaction, but especially after you've closed, ask your clients what they wish would have gone better or what you could have done better. Ask your mentor and your broker if they have any feedback for you as well. When you get this feedback, try not to be defensive or to justify what you have done wrong or poorly.

- Take what they say and write it down so you can use it to improve. Try to think of what you should have done instead, and then implement that into your buyer or seller checklist. Make a plan for how you will handle it differently next time. Now, this is very important: Call the people who gave you that feedback and thank them for it.

  Tell them that you have implemented something in your system to fix it, and tell them how much you appreciate them for helping you improve your business. This will help them refer you to others, and it will also make them feel they were heard. This makes the bad experiences much less damaging for future relationships.

- As you are going over these items and improvements, be extremely careful not to fall into being a victim or feeling entitled. Take ownership of the mistake, but do not let it bog you down or hurt your confidence. Say something like, "I'm very proud of myself that I handled these other 120 items perfectly and that my clients had only two things they didn't like out of this process. I'm also proud of myself that I made changes to my business to ensure that those two things don't happen again."

- Give yourself a pat on the back. Most agents don't ask for feedback, let alone make changes based on that feedback. You are well on your way to creating a sales experience that will be unparalleled by your competitors.

- Now that you have done some self-evaluating, try to identify moments in your life where you are still being a victim and feeling entitled. Make a goal to create affirmations to replace these thoughts and to react differently in such moments.

  In some cases, it might be helpful to carry a small notepad, and when you catch yourself feeling entitled or a victim, write down what the thought is and then write down a positive replacement thought, and repeat the positive affirmation seven times. You can continue doing this indefinitely until you feel you've purged your mind of the constant rut of victimhood.

By taking these steps, agents will improve their processes with every closing and will continually improve their mindset and become empowered individuals, purging negative thoughts and unrealistic entitlement from their lives.

Conclusion

If you are able to improve your process and systems with every transaction, you will become a better, constantly improving REALTOR® and more reliable with every home you sell.

This will show in your professionalism, and your confidence will grow, visibly.

Doing this in conjunction with improving your mindset and becoming empowered will give you a presence and a reputation that will precede you with clients.

And your growing confidence and reputation will constantly open up opportunities for your further growth.

Chapter 29

Go Out and Do It

You have learned how to change your mindset and become empowered.

You have been given systems and tools to have a very successful business.

You have been shown how to run your real estate business from A to Z and how to treat present clients and past clients in a manner that will lead to new clients — and new friends.

We have also called you out and, hopefully, helped you realize where you are being a victim or feeling entitled in your personal and business life.

If you have not already done so, now is the time to take action. You have everything you need. No more excuses. It's time to take your career to the next level. So start today.

Knowing effective systems and efficient processes is great, but too much learning can be one of the biggest obstacles for many REALTORS® to overcome. If you become a learner more than a doer, you will never truly dive into success and prosperity.

Doing

Here's a story of someone who needed to become a doer rather than just a learner.

I started mentoring Adam before he became a REALTOR®.

He was a friend of mine who had seen my success and was hugely disappointed in his efforts to make it in the corporate world, despite his degree. He had a lot of drive and previously developed sales skills, so he asked me about becoming a successful REALTOR®.

I got him going on the right track from the beginning. Problem was, because of location, he had to join a different brokerage than mine (he was not in my state). For this reason, we could not attend training together, and I had to advise him on how to get training where he was.

Problems arose when he became addicted to training, as I've seen with so many agents over the years. They go to sales meetings, they learn a bunch of great stuff, and they try to implement what they've just learned. But before you know it, they are attending another online webinar or thinking something along the lines of, "I can't implement the stuff about the training until I've learned more about this or that. So I've got to start reading this book first."

This is similar to someone in college who's got a degree, but is terrified of the world and so continues to study to get advanced degrees — not to create opportunities, but simply to avoid taking the next step in their lives. Adam was stuck in training addiction.

After observing this for several months, and not wanting to insert myself too aggressively, I finally had to call him out on it. I said, "Quite frankly, Adam, if you keep going to these training sessions and not implementing what they say, you're going to wear your brain down with a million ideas. It's going to make it even harder to implement the good ones you already have."

I told him that at his very next training he should write down everything that seemed good for his business, and then to commit not to attend any more training or read any more articles. And then he should practice what he had learned in that recent training for several days.

Obviously, Adam is a friend of mine, and being older than me, our relationship has been big brother-little brother. So he did not follow his 'little brother's' advice immediately. Luckily, about two weeks later, his broker at the time called him in and had the exact same conversation with him.

Eventually, Adam took my advice, and he hardly ever attends sales training anymore. In this case, it's good. He doesn't need the training, and it certainly was not motivating him. Now whenever he feels the need to learn new things, I recommend that he read books instead of attending classes. We sometimes talk about him going to a major seminar, but never more than once a quarter.

In the end, Adam ended up implementing the principles from the very first book he read before he even became a REALTOR®. This, in combination with some of my systems and tools I had shared with him, helped him build a strong business through working his own database. The sad thing is, he had that book and me as resources several months before he started actually implementing those principles and practices.

The good news is, once he started working on these things, he saw that while his education helped him with planning and strategy, he quickly realized that being in the field and doing the work was what actually led to results.

Adam is now providing comfortably for his family. He and his wife each bought a new car last year, and he is branching out to leadership opportunities within his brokerage.

You Have the Tools You Need

Here's the point: If you've already studied this book and highlighted important sections, you have every tool you could possibly need to make a living in the real estate business. Is there still more to learn? Certainly. I've seen REALTORS® make $300,000, $400,000 or $500,000 a year doing half of what's taught in this book, even while not doing it very consistently.

For this reason, I recommend that you do not read another real estate book until you have started using and mastering the methods and techniques I've shared with you here.

I've seen this same pattern of "training/education addiction" with dozens of REALTORS® over the course of my career. For example, I recently coached Amy, an agent who has been in the industry for one year. When she and I met, Amy was about to pull the trigger on quitting, and I could not blame her. She had not made a sale yet. Her best friend had actually just bought a house but worked with a stranger instead of her, despite being fully aware that Amy was a REALTOR®. Amy was at a pretty low point, and she was working only about half an hour a day as a REALTOR®, despite not having another job.

As I started our first coaching session, nothing but excuses and justifications came out of her mouth. She is probably one of the biggest victims I've ever coached. But, surprise, surprise, she had attended over forty real estate training courses over the last year. Still, Amy claims she doesn't know what to do on a daily basis. She says she won't really know what to do until she has clients, and then she'll be busy.

I'm waiting to give her some tough love, which will sound like this: "You will never have any clients if all you do is learn how to get them and not take action. Are you willing to take action, Amy? If not, I recommend you get a full-time job and put real estate out of your mind indefinitely."

This might sound harsh, but I've wasted a lot of time with

agents over the years, and I can see the warning signs. She must wake up, or she's likely to waste another year of her life, lose confidence, and end up in a tough financial situation.

On a positive note, I'd like to tell you a story about a REALTOR® named Ted. In my previous company, there was a sales training course put on by a local lender. It was a fairly comprehensive course and took several weeks to complete. I met Ted while he was attending this course, thinking it was his first time through. As I got to know him better, I learned that he had not yet sold a home, he had been a REALTOR® for six months, and this was his third time going through that course.

Knocking on Doors

I called Ted's broker and asked her what the situation was. She expressed to me her frustration that Ted was going to keep attending these trainings and never sell a home. "I'm sure he will quit in a year," she said. I called Ted and expressed to him my concern that he was wasting afternoons attending the same training again. I was very straightforward and told him his broker and I had discussed this, and that I had seen other REALTORS® quit real estate after continuing in the cycle he was in. I was able to convince Ted to go out and knock on some doors with me.

Ted knew everything about knocking on doors. He knew the script. He knew what systems to use to follow up. He had even chosen a great area, with a price range that ensured a lot of turnover. Obviously, he had learned all these things in the training he'd been attending. When we got to the first door, Ted froze up and told me he did not know what to say. Just as the homeowner opened the door, I stepped in and purposely moved forward with the simplest script possible.

I said, "Hello, my name is Brian. How are you doing?" They said they were doing well. "I'm a local REALTOR®," I said. "I'm hoping to find people who would be interested in selling their home. Have you considered selling your home anytime soon?" The conversation was friendly but not very long, as they'd moved in only two years ago.

As we were walking away, I told Ted, "I have never used that script before. I purposely used something new to demonstrate to you how easy it is. It is now time to take action. You've learned a lot, but at this point, the only important thing is that you knock on the door."

One hour later, we had a listing appointment scheduled, and by the end of the week Ted had his first listing. In the next six months, he sold four homes. The momentum he has built to this point will likely lead Ted to selling anywhere between twelve and fifteen homes next year, which is three times more than the average REALTOR® in his market sells.

It is important to mention here that, although I have told several stories of people who needed to stop attending training, I still recommend that you keep your skills sharp, especially when it comes to legal issues within the industry. For an experienced agent who is out working and succeeding, one or two training sessions a month is still good practice. Just make sure it is on topics that you have little to no knowledge about.

Your Next Steps RIGHT NOW

- Skim through this book and reread the portions you highlighted. This should serve as a reminder of what was important to you the first time around, and hopefully you are already doing some of them. If not, this is your wakeup call. How long ago did you highlight that section without taking action? Does an excuse come to mind? Are you a victim?

- If you have not already done so, create a daily schedule and stick to it 100%. For example, if you want to wake up at 6 a.m. every day, don't make weekends an exception. If you stay up some nights, still wake up at 6 a.m. the next morning, even if it means you need to take a nap later. Keep to a strict schedule.

- Within that same line of thinking, you need a similar goal of how late you'll work every day. Too many agents, once they have become organized and focused, will accomplish their to-do lists at 2 p.m. and take the rest of the day off. Or they will foolishly waste time chatting with colleagues. You need to stay productive throughout the day and stick to the schedule you created. If you need to chat, do so after your scheduled work hours.

- On the subject of water-cooler talk, make it your goal and your constant discipline to never waste more than two or three minutes on a conversation with a colleague. Many agents rush off the phone with clients because they feel they have important work to do, and then they spend an hour complaining about the same client to their coworkers.

- You need to start acting as if you have a boss, and that boss is yourself . If you were the boss of yourself and saw how you spend the day, would you be pleased with your work ethic, or would you fire yourself, and replace yourself with someone who knows how to put in a full day's work without giving in to distractions?

- Once you've mastered these things, be sure to use your yellow pad with the To-Do List you check off daily and, if necessary (and I highly recommend this), time-blocking your schedule. Stay disciplined regarding that time-blocking. As REALTORS®, our days can get away from us very easily, no matter how well we do on these steps. For that reason, stay disciplined every day to make up for those rare instances where the deal takes all your time, or you need to put out flames for a transaction over the course of several days.

- <u>Do not forget your affirmations.</u> If you think you have somehow arrived and you don't need to continue using positive affirmations, you are seriously kidding yourself. Some of the most successful and positive people in the world did not just become that way because of affirmations. But they stay that way because they still constantly use their basic affirmations.

- I cannot tell you how many influencers I have heard talk about how they constantly need affirmations to keep from falling back into old habits and losing confidence in themselves. ***And these are people who speak on stage, inspire others, and who have fans who want to be like them.***

- Make sure you review your goals and numbers at least once a month and check to see if you are on track to hit them. Do a quarterly review of your performance and projection. if you're not on pace, make changes — create new approaches, work more hours, and resolve conflicts that are distracting you from your work.

- Do not become so hyper-focused on your business and yourself that you lose the willingness to serve. Oftentimes, the best way to generate business is to serve and make it a goal to do something each day to help someone else succeed, even competitors in the office. This will come back tenfold to you as people reciprocate your kindness, and good karma comes back to you.

Conclusion

You are capable of greatness.

You now have the tools to make $1 million a year — or more. Many of you might not make it there. But you can at least double or triple your current income and achieve the success that has seemed so elusive to you in the past.

This is your time to shine!

Odds are, your results will be even better than you had hoped for when you started your satisfying, fascinating, and very rewarding journey in the field of real estate.